LAST FLIGHT

LAST FLIGHT

by Amelia Earhart

Arranged by George Palmer Putnam

Foreword by Walter J. Boyne

ORION BOOKS
NEW YORK

Grateful acknowledgment is made to *This Week* for permission to reprint the poem by Nathalia Crane.

Introduction copyright © 1988 by Crown Publishers, Inc.
Copyright 1937 by Harcourt, Brace and Company, Inc. Copyright © renewed 1964 by Mrs. George Palmer Putnam.

Published by Orion Books, a division of Crown Publishers, Inc., 225 Park Avenue South, New York, New York 10003 and represented in Canada by the Canadian MANDA Group

CROWN, ORION and Colophon are trademarks of Crown Publishers, Inc.

Manufactured in the United States of America

Library of Congress Cataloging-in-Publication Data

Earhart, Amelia, 1897–1937.
    Last flight.

    Originally published: New York: Harcourt, Brace, © 1937.
    1. Aeronautics—Flights. 2. Earhart, Amelia,
1897–1937. 3. Putnam, George Palmer, 1887–1950.
II. Title.
TL721 · E3A3   1988   629 · 13 ' 092 ' 4   87–7291

ISBN 0-517-56794-6

10 9 8 7 6 5 4 3 2 1

First Edition

TO FLOYD
with gratitude
for all-weather friendship

He ne'er is crowned
With immortality—who fears to follow
Where airy voices lead.

KEATS

AMELIA EARHART

Emptied is old Lorenzo's royal crypt;
Breathless now stands the startled Taj Mahal;
Amelia lies in that blue manuscript—
The sea, true heroine's memorial.
So she achieves. What if the fatal prize
Be misty tomb with airy marble set?
Who knows where Desdemona's kerchief lies,
Or where the last word of dark Juliet?
A sudden courage plucks us from ourselves,
Bids us be heroine though death the price;
Wherefore we bed on many lilied shelves
The straight defenders of the sacrifice.
   Count her among the beautiful and brave,
   Her turquoise mausoleum in each wave.

NATHALIA CRANE

Contents

Foreword

Few women have captured the imagination of the American public as Amelia Earhart did. None have held on to it longer. More than half a century has passed since her disappearance in the South Pacific in July 1937, and each succeeding year brings forth new books on her and her probable fate. The speculations—or, for the true believer, the facts—about the dangerous last flight in her Lockheed Electra cover an extraordinary range. Some make dramatic claims that she was on a "cold-war reconnaissance" mission analagous to that of Gary Powers, another pilot in a later Lockheed. Others, less romantic, believe simply that she had attempted more than she and her navigator, Fred Noonan, were capable of achieving.

Ultimately, as time passes and the circumstances surrounding her last flight become less sensitive for nations and for individuals, the actual events will be revealed. If there are secret records that conceal a gigantic government conspiracy in which she played a willing part, time will permit their disclosure. If, when all the possible files are opened, there is nothing to indicate government involvement, a conclusion can be drawn that she suffered the fate of so many flyers of her day: valiant submission to great odds.

It undoubtedly would be fitting to know what happened to her, and to recognize appropriately any contribution she made to our nation's security. Mere knowledge of her fate, however, would add little to her stature as the first American woman to be widely acknowledged as a pilot first and a woman second. She was preceded by such great women flyers as Harriet Quimby and Katherine Stinson and followed by others such as Jacqueline Cochran and Jena Yeager. But her status remains unique, for a variety of reasons.

Perhaps least important of these was her almost familial resemblance to Charles Lindbergh. It was a gift of God to the press to have a famous, attractive, daring woman flyer who just happened to look like the greatest male aviation hero of the time. The fact that neither Earhart nor Lindbergh cared for the comparison mattered not at all.

More important was that the public understood that she and she alone, was doing the flying, in airplanes exactly like those that men were using. There could be no condescension to a woman setting records solo in a Lockheed Vega when praise was being heaped upon men like Wiley Post and Jimmy Mattern for their exploits in the same airplane. Her instincts were correct. Flying as a passenger in the Fokker *Friendship* had been a galling experience, and she immediately discounted the praise that was heaped upon her. In her subsequent flights—solo across the Atlantic, across the United States, and from Hawaii to California—she was determined to make the public see that in the ability to fly, a woman was fully equal to a man.

That she succeeded in this is attested to by the organizations, the International Forest of Friendship and the group she helped found, the International 99s, which actively continue to honor her. And this brings us to the last and greatest mystery about Amelia Earhart: the failure of the great movements for women's rights to make full use of her legend and her example.

Amelia Earhart was in advance of her time by ten years in aviation and by two generations in promoting women's rights. Yet her contributions were all but overlooked by the most potent political elements of the time. This failure was a tremendous loss, for in Amelia Earhart women had a sensitive, powerful champion. She understood instinctively that the press and public must be relentlessly courted, yet that a distance had to be preserved and an image maintained. In the thousands of feet of motion picture film, in the millions of photographs of her, there comes across an intelligent, knowing woman, one who would have prospered mightily in the 1970s and 1980s as a symbol as potent as that of Joan of Arc in the crusade for women's rights.

Perhaps it does not matter. The real results of her legacy are all around us. The most obvious examples are in aviation. Airlines actively recruit women for positions as pilots (how she would have loved that), and there are many women serving as military crew members. Crews composed entirely of women—pilots, navigators, flight engineer, loadmaster and crew chief—routinely fly huge Air Force jet transports everywhere around the world. In the Netherlands, women have been accepted as combat pilots, and there are those who seek the same role for them in the United States' armed forces.

Amelia Earhart came perhaps before her time, but the image this book conveys so well, that of the smiling, confident, capable, yet compassionate human being, is one of which we can all be proud.

Walter J. Boyne
Reston, Virginia
1987

Introduction

This is the story of "Last Flight." It was to have been called "World Flight," but fate willed otherwise. It is written almost entirely by Amelia Earhart herself.

We have her narrative of the journey all the way around the world to New Guinea, as it came by cable and telephone. Many of those accounts she supplemented with further notes which arrived later by letter. Likewise she sent back the log-books of the journey, their pages filled with her own penciling, scribbled in the cockpit as she flew over four continents.

There is, too, her own commencement of "World Flight." She had promised her publishers the manuscript promptly; that was one of the chores she accepted to make possible her ambition. So when she was turned back from Honolulu by the accident there in March, she did what she could to get the book well launched. To all that is added some material from others, who knew her and wrote about her.

Weaving all this together, I have sought to make a simple record of A. E.'s last adventure for myself and for the many who loved her and found cheer in her gallant, friendly life.

When time has smoothed out somewhat the rough sorrows of the present, there will be another book—the full story of Amelia Earhart's life. That's a project for a tomorrow of retrospect.

Through the rich years of our work and play together, there was often a cloud hanging overhead—the shadow of danger. It was not, mind you, always an ominous cloud, but rather one somehow lined with a gay silver of understanding.

A.E. recognized its presence more frankly than I.

"Some day," she would say, "I'll get bumped off. There's so much to do, so much fun here, I don't want to go, but . . ."

In the preparation for her flights, she recognized the risks. But in the hazards of "living dangerously" she seemed more concerned for others than for herself.

She often said that on her solo Atlantic flight her chances of success were "one in ten." And on the Honolulu–Oakland hop, "fifty-fifty." What percentage she reckoned on this world flight I do not know. I do know that always, where her flying brought cause for fear, I was the frightened one.

"The time to worry," she declared, "is three months before a flight. Decide then whether or not the goal is worth the risks involved. If it is, stop worrying. To worry is to add another hazard. It retards reactions, makes one unfit. Hamlet," she'd add with that infectious grin, "would have been a bad aviator. He worried too much."

This journey around the world was to be her last "record" flight. Before she left Oakland in March for Honolulu, A. E. confided to a friend what she had already told me. . . . Seemingly there will be no more flights for her, of any kind. All reasonable evidence now points to that. Yet, unreasonably, hope lingers that the Providence which guarded her so often may still deliver her back in some miraculous manner.

Among many poignant memories, two stand out. At San Francisco we looked out, one evening, at the Pacific. Again, from our hotel window in Miami, we saw the sun rise on the Atlantic. Each time A. E. gazed silently for a time. And each time her words were almost the same.

"It's a very big ocean—*so* much water!" She spoke with a little sigh which promptly dissipated into a reassuring chuckle.

I asked if she could not give up the project. Life held so much else. Her reply is clear in my mind:

"Please don't be concerned. It just seems that I must try this flight. I've weighed it all carefully. With it behind me life will be fuller and richer. I can be content. Afterward it will be fun to grow old."

I think, somehow, she knew. Whatever came to pass, the contentment she sought was assured.

"When I go," she often said, "I'd like best to go in my plane. Quickly."

So this is not a chronicle of regret, but of high and happy adventure. That is as she would have her book. May its pages convey some measure of the pervading charm and magic character of Amelia Earhart, whose explorings were as much of the mind and spirit as of the air.

G. P. P.

LAST FLIGHT

A Pilot Grows Up

Pilots are always dreaming dreams.

My dream, of owning a multi-motored plane, probably first took form in May 1935.

I was flying nonstop from Mexico City to New York. The straight line course, from Tampico to New Orleans, took me over about seven hundred miles of the Gulf of Mexico. There weren't many clouds, so for once what lay below was quite visible. It did seem a good deal of water.

Previously I'd been by air twice across the North Atlantic, and once from Hawaii to California. All three voyages were flown chiefly at night, with heavy clouds during most of the daylight hours. So in the combined six thousand miles or more of previous over-ocean flying it happened I'd seen next to nothing of ocean.

Given daylight and good visibility, the Gulf of Mexico looked large. And wet. One's imagination toyed with the thought of what would happen if the single engine of the Lockheed Vega should conk. Not that my faithful Wasp ever had failed me, or indeed, even protested mildly. But, at that, the very finest machinery *could* develop indigestion.

So, on that sunny morning out of sight of land, I promised my lovely red Vega I'd fly her across no more water. And I promised myself that any further over-ocean flying would be attempted in a plane with more than one motor, capable of keeping aloft with a single engine. Just in case.

Which, in a way, was for me the beginning of the world flight project. Where to find the tree on which costly airplanes grow, I did not know. But I did know the kind I wanted—an Electra Lockheed, big brother of my Vegas, with, of course, Wasp engines.

Such is the trusting simplicity of a pilot's mind, it seemed ordained that somehow the dream would materialize. Once the prize was in hand, obviously there was one flight which I most wanted to attempt—a circumnavigation of the globe as near its waistline as could be.

Before writing about the preparation for that flight, and of the journey itself, it seems well to set down briefly the career, such as it is, of a girl who grew up to love flying—the who, when and why of this particular pilot.

At the age of ten I saw my first airplane. It was sitting in a slightly enclosed area at the Iowa State Fair in Des Moines. It was a thing of rusty wire and wood and looked not at all interesting. One of the grown-ups who happened to be around pointed it out to me and said: "Look, dear, it flies." I looked as directed but confess I was much more interested in an absurd hat made of an inverted peach-basket which I had just purchased for fifteen cents.

What psychoanalysts would make of this incident, in the light of subsequent behavior, I do not know. Today I loathe hats for more than a few minutes on the head and am sure I should pass by the niftiest creation if an airplane were anywhere around.

The next airplane which impinged upon my consciousness was about the time of the armistice. Again I found myself at a Fair, this time the great exposition held at Toronto in Canada. A young woman friend and I had gone to the Fair grounds to see an exhibition of stunt flying by one of the aces returned from the war. These men were the heroes of the hour. They were in demand at social teas, and to entertain crowds by giving stunting exhibitions. The airplanes they rode so gallantly to fame were as singular as they. For aviation in those days was very limited. About all a pilot could do was to joy-hop. That is (1) taking a few hardy passengers for short rides; (2) teaching even hardier students to fly; and (3) giving exhibitions.

The idea that airplanes could be transportation as today entered nobody's noggin.

My friend and I, in order to see the show, planted ourselves in the middle of a clearing. We watched a small plane turn and twist in the air, black against the sky excepting when the afternoon sun caught the scarlet of its wings. After fifteen or twenty minutes of stunting, the pilot began to dive at the crowd. Looking back as a pilot I think I understand why. He was bored. He had looped and rolled and spun and finished his little bag of tricks, and there was nothing left to do but watch the people on the ground running as he swooped close to them.

Pilots, in 1918, to relieve the monotony of never going anywhere, rolled their wheels on the top of moving freight trains; flew so low over boats that the terrified occupants lay flat on the deck; or they dived at crowds on the beach or at picnics. Today of course the Department of Commerce would ground a pilot for such antics.

I am sure the sight of two young women alone made a tempting target for the pilot. I am sure he said to himself, "Watch me make them scamper."

After a few attempts one did but the other stood her ground. I remember the mingled fear and pleasure which surged over me as I watched that small plane at the top of its earthward swoop. Common sense told me if something went wrong with the mechanism, or if the pilot lost control, he, the airplane and I would be rolled up in a ball together. I did not understand it at the time but I believe that little red airplane said something to me as it swished by.

I worked in a hospital during the war. From that experience I decided that medicine interested me most. Whether or not medicine needed me I did not question. So I enrolled at Columbia University in New York and started in to do the peculiar things they do who would be physicians. I fed orange juice to mice and dissected cockroaches. I have never seen a cockroach since but I remember that the creature has an extraordinarily large brain.

However, I could not forget airplanes.

I went to California for a summer vacation and found air meets, as distinct from wartime exhibitions, just beginning. I went to every one and finally one day came a chance to ride. Frank Hawks took me on the first hop. He was then a barnstorming pilot on the west coast, unknown to the fame he later acquired. By the time I had got two or three hundred feet off the ground I knew I had to fly.

I think my mother realized before I did how much airplanes were beginning to mean to me, for she helped me buy the first one. It was second-hand, painted bright yellow, and one of the first light airplanes developed in this country. The motor was so rough that my feet went to sleep after more than a few minutes on the rudder bar. I had a system of lending the plane for demonstration so as not to be charged storage. Hangar rental would have annihilated my salary.

After a year my longest hop was from Long Beach to Pasadena, about 40 miles. Still I all but set off to cross the continent by air. The fact that I couldn't buy gasoline myself forced me to compromise and drive a car with Mother along. I am sure I wouldn't be here to tell the tale if I had carried out the original plan.

I did what flying I could afford in the next few years and then the "Friendship" came along. I was working in Denison House in Boston, one of America's oldest social settlements.

"Phone for you, Miss Earhart."

"Tell 'em I'm busy." At the moment I was the center of an eager swarm of Chinese and Syrian neighborhood children, piling in for games and classes.

"Says it's important."

So I excused myself and went to listen to a man's voice asking me whether I was interested in doing something dangerous in the air. At first I thought the conversation was a joke and said so. Several times before I had been approached by bootleggers who promised rich reward and no danger—"Absolutely no danger to you, Leddy."

The frank admission of risk stirred my curiosity. References were demanded and supplied. Good references. An appointment was arranged for that evening.

"Would you like to fly the Atlantic?"

My reply was a prompt "Yes"—provided the equipment was all right and the crew capable. Nine years ago flying oceans was less commonplace than today, and my own experience as a pilot was limited to a few hundred hours in small planes which work and finances permitted.

So I went to New York and met the man entrusted with the quaint commission of finding a woman willing to fly the Atlantic. The candidate, I gathered, should be a flyer herself, with social graces, education, charm and, perchance, pulchritude.

His appraisal left me discomforted. Somehow this seeker for feminine perfection seemed unimpressed. Anyway, I showed my pilot's license (it happened to be the first granted an American woman by the F.A.I.) and inwardly prepared to start back for Boston.

But he felt that, having come so far, I might as well meet the representatives of Mrs. Frederick Guest, whose generosity was making the flight possible, and at whose insistence a woman was to be taken along. Those representatives were David T. Layman, Jr., and John S. Phipps, before which masculine jury I made my next appearance. It should have been slightly embarrassing, for if I were found wanting in too many ways I would be counted out. On the other hand, if I were just too fascinating, the gallant gentlemen might be loath to risk drowning me. Anyone could see the meeting was a crisis.

A few days later the verdict came. The flight actually would be made and I could go if I wished. Naturally I couldn't say "No." Who would refuse an invitation to such a shining adventure?

Followed, in due course, after weeks of mechanical preparation, efforts to get the monoplane "Friendship" off from the gray waters of Boston Harbor. There were chill before-dawn gettings-up, with breakfasts snatched and thermos bottles filled at an all-night lunch counter. Brief voyages on the tugboat *Sadie Ross* to the anchored plane, followed by the sputter of the motors awakening to Mechanic Lou Gordon's coaxing and their later full-throated roar when Pilot "Bill" Stultz gave them the gun—and I crouched on the fuselage floor hoping we were really off.

Thrice we failed, dragging back to Boston for more long days of waiting. Waiting is apt to be so much harder than *going,* with the excitement of movement, of getting off, of adventure-around-the-corner.

Finally one morning the "Friendship" took off successfully, and Stultz, Gordon, and I transferred ourselves to Newfoundland. After thirteen days of weary waiting at Trepassey (how well I remember the alternating diet of mutton and rabbits!) the Atlantic flight started. Twenty hours and forty minutes later we tied up to a buoy off Burryport, Wales. I recall desperately waving a towel; one friendly soul ashore pulled off his coat and waved back. But beyond that for an hour nothing happened. It took persistence to arouse interest in an itinerant trans-Atlantic plane.

I myself did no piloting on that trip. But I gained experience. In London I was introduced to Lady Mary Heath, the then very active Irish woman flyer. She had just made a record flight from London to Cape Town and I purchased the small plane she had used. It wore on its chest a number of medals given her at various stops she made on the long route.

After the pleasant accident of being the first woman to cross the Atlantic by air, I was launched into a life full of interest. Aviation offered such fun as crossing the continent in planes large and small, trying the whirling rotors of an autogiro, making record flights. With these activities came opportunity to know women everywhere who shared my conviction that there is so much women can do in the modern world and should be permitted to do irrespective of their sex. Probably my greatest satisfaction was to indicate by example now and then, that women can sometimes do things themselves if given the chance.

Here I should add that the "Friendship" flight brought me something even dearer than such opportunities. That Man-who-was-to-find-a-girl-to-fly-the-Atlantic, who found me and then managed the flight, was George Palmer Putnam. In 1931 we married. Mostly, my flying has been solo, but the preparation for it wasn't. Without my husband's help and encouragement I could not have attempted what I have. Ours has been a contented and reasonable partnership, he with his solo jobs and I with mine. But always with work and play together, conducted under a satisfactory system of dual control.

I was hardly home when I started off to fly the continent—my 1924 ambition four years late. Lady Heath's plane was very small. It had folding wings so that it actually could fit in a garage. I cranked the motor by standing behind the propeller and pulling it down with one hand. The plane was so light I could pick it up by the tail and drag it easily around the field.

At that time I was full of missionary zeal for the cause of aviation. I refused to wear the high-bred aviation togs of the moment. Instead I simply wore a dress or suit. I carried no chute and instead of a helmet used a close-fitting hat. I stepped into the airplane with as much nonchalance as I could muster, hoping that onlookers would be persuaded that flying was nothing more than an everyday occurrence. I refused even to wear goggles, obviously. However, I put them on as I taxied to the end of the field and wore them while flying, being sure to take them off shortly after I landed.

That was thoroughly informal flying. Pilots landed in pastures, race courses, even golf links where they were still enough of a novelty to be welcome.

In those days domestic animals scurried to the fancied protection of trees and barns when the flying monsters roared above them. Now along the airways there's not enough curiosity left for a self-respecting cow even to lift her head to see what goes on in the sky. She's just bored. Stories of that happy-go-lucky period should be put together in a saga to regale the scientific, precision flyers of tomorrow.

Nineteen-twenty-nine was the year of the women's derby from California to Cleveland, the first time a cross-country race had ever been sponsored for women alone. I felt I needed a new plane for this extraordinary sporting event. So I traded in the faithful little Avion for my first Lockheed Vega. It was a third-hand clunk but to me a heavenly chariot.

I crossed the continent again from New York to California to stop at the Lockheed factory. I thought possibly there might be a few adjustments necessary before I entered the race. There I met the great Wiley Post for the first time. Wiley Post had not then had his vision of stratosphere flying, and was simply a routine check pilot in the employ of the Lockheed company.

It fell to him to take my airplane up for test. Having circled the field once, he came down and proceeded to tell everyone within earshot that my lovely airplane was the foulest he had ever flown. Of course the worse he made the plane, the better pilot I became. The fact that I should have been able to herd such a hopeless piece of mechanism across the continent successfully was the one bright spot in the ensuing half hour.

Finally Lockheed officials were so impressed by my prowess (or so sorry for me) that they traded me a brand new plane. The clunk was never flown again.

The Derby produced one of the gems which belong in the folklore of aviation. Something went wrong with her motor and Ruth Elder made a forced landing in a field thickly inhabited by cattle. The bovine population crowded around her plane and proceeded to lick the paint off the wings—there seemed to be something in the "doped" finish that appealed to them. Meanwhile, Ruth snuggled down in the safety of the cockpit. "You see," she explained, "I didn't know much about such things and was uncertain as to the sex of the visitors. My plane was red—very red. And I'd always heard what bulls did to *that*." . . . Apparently the cows were cows.

After the "Friendship" flight I did not immediately plan to fly the Atlantic alone. But later as I gained in experience and looked back over the years I decided that I had had enough to try to make it solo. Lockheed #2 was then about three years old. It had been completely reconditioned and a new and larger engine put in. By the spring of 1932 plane and pilot were ready.

Oddly, one of my clearest memories of the Atlantic solo concerns not the flight itself but my departure from home. On May 19th the weather outlook was so unpromising we had abandoned hope of getting off that day. So I had driven in to New York from our home in Westchester. Just before noon an urgent message caught up with me immediately to get in touch with Mr. Putnam at the Weather Bureau.

Our phone conversation was brief.

"It looks like the break we've waited for," he said. "Doc Kimball says this afternoon is fine to get to Newfoundland—St. John's anyway. And by tomorrow the Atlantic looks as good as you're likely to get it for some time."

I asked a few questions. A threatening "low" on the first leg of the route had dissipated to the southeast; a "high" seemed to be moving in promisingly beyond Newfoundland.

"Okeh! We'll start," I said. Mr. Putnam agreed he would corral Bernt Balchen, my technical adviser who was to go with me to Newfoundland to be sure that everything was as right as could be before I hopped off. I explained I would have to rush back to Rye to get my flying clothes and maps. We arranged to meet at two o'clock at the city end of the George Washington Bridge, which leads across the Hudson toward Teterboro Airport in New Jersey, where my plane waited.

At fast as I dared—traffic cops being what they are—I drove the twenty-five miles to Rye. Five minutes was enough to pick up my things. Plus a lingering few more to drink in the beauty of a lovely treasured sight. Beside and below our bedroom windows were dog-wood trees, their blossoms in luxuriant full flower, unbelievable bouquets of white and pink flecked with the sunshine of spring. Those sweet blooms smiled at me a radiant farewell. . . . That is a memory I have never forgotten.

Looking back, there are less cheering recollections of that night over the Atlantic. Of seeing, for instance, the flames lick through the exhaust collector ring and wondering, in a detached way, whether one would prefer drowning to incineration. Of the five hours of storm, during black midnight, when I kept right side up by instruments alone, buffeted about as I never was before. Of much beside, not the least the feeling of fine loneliness and of realization that the machine I rode was doing its best and required from me the best I had.

And one further fact of the flight, which I've not set down in words before. I carried a barograph, an instrument which records on a disc the course of the plane, its rate of ascent and descent, its levels of flight all co-ordinated with clocked time. My tell-tale disc could tell a tale. At one point it recorded an almost vertical drop of three thousand feet. It started at an altitude of something over 3,000 feet, and ended—well, something above the water. That happened when the plane suddenly "iced up" and went into a spin. How long we spun I do not know. I do know that I tried my best to do exactly what one should do with a spinning plane, and regained flying control as the warmth of the lower altitude melted the ice. As we righted and held level again, through the blackness below I could see the white-caps too close for comfort.

All that was five full years ago, a long time to recall little things. So I wonder if Bernt Balchen remembers as I do the three words he said to me as I left Harbor Grace. They were: "Okeh. So-long. Good luck."

First Pacific Flight

While this is to be a record of the round-the-world voyage, now that I've referred to the Atlantic flights I would like to tell here also the story of the trip from Hawaii to California. Contrasted to the Atlantic crossings, that was a journey of stars, not storms; of tropic loveliness instead of ice.

While I used the same type airplane on the Pacific flight as on the Atlantic, and the identical Wasp motor (bless its heart!), still I had improved equipment for the latter trip.

For instance, my plumbing system, by which I mean the metal fuel lines, was entirely encased in rubber tubing—double insurance against possible leak of precious fuel. Then I had a controllable pitch propeller. The controllable pitch propeller works as does the gear shift in your car. A flyer takes off in low, climbs to the altitude at which he wishes to fly, shifts into high, and away he goes. The propeller facilitates taking off with heavy loads, and gives greater speed in the air. Of course speed is a very definite safety factor when flying over dangerous areas, or over long stretches of water in a land plane.

Your little geographies told you that the northeast trade winds blow steadily in the mid-Pacific region. They do, excepting on the day I planned to take off. Then the winds switched around to the south and southwest and blew steadily from that direction.

Early on the morning of January 11, 1935, the clouds began to gather over Honolulu and by eleven a tropical downpour was in full force. I was assured it was very unusual weather. The military airport from which I planned to take off has no hard-surface runways and I knew that if I left that afternoon, as planned, I should have to lift my heavy load from very soggy ground. Wheeler Field then was about six thousand feet long, laid out in the direction of the prevailing winds, which refused to prevail.

The Army had very kindly mowed a pathway for me in the long grass and planted little white flags along both edges to facilitate my taking off in a straight line. So effective was that planting of white flags that I used the same system later in the take-off from Mexico City where we fashioned a home-made runway on the baked surface of a dry lake-bed.

At one o'clock conditions were no better; nor at two, nor at three. Following luncheon at an Army officer's home we kept our noses flattened against the windowpane, watching the weather. At 3:30 the rain definitely slackened and it looked as if the clouds might lift. So I hied me down to the hangar, in which my plane was housed, to look the situation over. I found the field soaked; and the spirits of the faithful few who were standing by, very damp indeed. However, I asked the men to get the plane out, to put in the few remaining gallons of gas the tanks would hold, to stow all my equipment (including a prized rubber boat) and to warm up the motor. I felt a take-off later in the day was possible and I wished the plane ready in every detail.

I must say something about the plane which has been my companion aloft for so many flying hours. It was a craft to delight the eye, its wings and fuselage painted red with gold stripes down the side. Possibly it may have seemed a trifle gaudy on the ground but I am sure it looked lovely against one of those white clouds. It was a closed plane. I drive a closed car and fly a closed plane. I don't like to be mussed up. Further, the added comfort of a closed plane very definitely lessens fatigue, and fatigue must be considered when one is preparing for a long flight. The Vega normally carries six passengers and the pilot, the passengers in the rear, the pilot in front perched in a cockpit overlooking the motor with its 500 horses. The six passenger seats had been replaced by large fuel tanks capable of carrying 520 gallons of gasoline. There are no service stations between Honolulu and the United States!

My cockpit was a very cozy little cubbyhole. I sat on a cushion just large enough for me. On the right-hand side of the seat was a large black box, the radio, with the dials on top so I could reach them easily. On the left was a large compass and two pump handles, pumps which enabled me to change fuel from one set of tanks to the other. Some of the fuel was carried in the wing, which is the normal position in commercial craft, and some in the cabin tanks. In case my motor-driven pump should fail I could still keep going by using that hand system. I have had to pump as long as six hours on occasion, which is pretty tiring. But it is well worth having that emergency system.

In a little cupboard in the wing, to the right, I carried provisions. I don't drink tea or coffee so I had none with me. On the Atlantic flight I had a thermos bottle of hot soup, but it did not work out very well, so from Honolulu I carried a thermos bottle of hot chocolate. Then I had malted milk tablets, sweet chocolate, tomato juice, and water. One of the Army officer's wives thought I was starting out on a 2,400-mile journey with entirely too little to eat so she asked if she couldn't put up a picnic lunch for me. I told her that for some reason or other it was always difficult for me on a long flight to eat much food, but if she packed a lunch I would take it with me. So I had that too.

On the left side there was another little cabinet in which were stored my tools. I don't use hairpins so I have to carry regular tools! Also, there were extra fuses, extra flashlight, pad and pencils, rags, string, odds and ends that might come in handy.

After I asked the men to warm up the motor, I went over to the Weather Bureau for a final check and found that if I did not leave that afternoon, despite local conditions, I would be held indefinitely by storms coming in over the Pacific. So about 4:30 I returned to the plane, which was sitting out on the concrete apron. The motor purred sweetly. I crawled into the cockpit and tested it myself. It sounded perfect. So I told the men to take away the blocks in front of the wheels.

I turned the plane and headed for the take-off pathway, my mechanic running along beside it. I could see him out of the cockpit window and observed that with every step he took the mud squashed up to his shoe tops, so soft was the ground. My mechanic was very gloomy, his cigarette hanging out of the corner of his mouth, his face as white as his coveralls. I wanted to call, "Cheer up, Ernie! It will soon be over." But of course I couldn't make him hear over the sound of the motor.

Glancing to the left, I noticed three fire engines drawn up in front of the hangars, and one ambulance. The Army to a man seemed to have those little squirt fire extinguishers, and the women present had their handkerchiefs out, obviously ready for any emergency.

The take-off with an excessive fuel load is the most hazardous moment, if such could be determined, because of the possibility of fire if anything goes amiss. But please do not compare such a take-off with those of ordinary everyday flying. It is no more fair to compare the two than it is to compare automobile racing and safe automobile driving—if such there be!

When my mechanic had pried loose a great ball of mud and grass that had caked up on the tail skid, I put the plane in take-off position, looked down the long pathway ahead of me, and beyond to the sugarcane fields stretching to the crest of the mountains which cross the island diagonally. Those mountains usually are sharp in outline but that day they were softened by low-hanging gray clouds.

From the little flags hanging limply on their sticks I saw that what wind I had was with me. That was a disadvantage. You realize a plane takes off against the wind, not with it, just as a small boy flies his kite. He doesn't run with the wind to get his kite into the air, but runs against it. Of course an airplane is simply a kite with a motor instead of the small boy.

I pushed the throttle ahead. The Vega started to move and gather speed. I felt the tail come up. The plane got lighter and lighter on the wheels. After rolling about two thousand feet a large bump on the surface of the field threw the plane completely off the ground. I pushed the throttle ahead to the farthest notch, and gave her all the power I had. The plane started to settle, then caught—and we were off.

I have often been asked what I think about at the moment of take-off. Of course no pilot sits and feels his pulse as he flies. He has to be part of the machine. If he thinks of anything but the task in hand then trouble is probably just around the corner.

Although I had plenty to do immediately after that take-off, some impressions of the moments that followed remain vivid in my memory.

I realized that at one time I was flying over a forbidden area at a forbidden altitude. The islands are dotted with military reservations over which civilian aircraft may not fly under a certain altitude; and as I was climbing slowly with my heavy load I was definitely under the prescribed limit. I wondered in a third-person kind of way whether the Navy (it was a Naval reservation) would begin taking pot-shots at me, or whether they would have me arrested when I arrived, wherever I arrived, if I arrived.

My course lay over the edge of Honolulu. As I flew by that lovely city and realized it was just about the close of the business day, the thought flashed through my mind that everyone was going home to supper—but me.

It was just five o'clock as I passed over Makapuu Point, the last island outpost on my course. Shortly afterward I let down my radio antenna and sent my first message, something like this: "Flying 6,000 feet, through scattered clouds, temperature outside 50 degrees. Everything okeh."

I was tuned in at the time to a musical program on KGU, the commercial broadcast station in Honolulu. I wasn't listening to the music as such, but simply keeping the station tuned in so that when word came for me, as arranged beforehand, I could increase the volume and understand what was said. Suddenly I heard the music stop and the announcer's voice say, "We are interrupting our musical program with an important news flash. Amelia Earhart has just taken off from Honolulu on an attempted flight to Oakland."

Telling me!

Then the announcer's voice continued: "Mr. Putnam will try to communicate with his wife." Then I heard my husband's voice as if he were in the next room saying: "A. E., the noise of your motor interferes with your broadcast. Will you please try to speak a little louder so we can hear you." It was thrilling to have his voice come in so clear to me, sitting out there over the Pacific. It was really one of the high points of the flight.

Clouds were all about me from the start. I had to climb 6,000 feet to get over the first layers of filmy white. I could look down and see the water, dark blue and then darker blue, then black, as night came on.

It was a night of stars. Stars hung outside my cockpit window near enough to touch. I have never seen so many or such large ones. I

14

shall never forget the contrast of the white clouds and the moonlight and starlight against the black of the sea. It is interesting that I have flown over thousands of miles of water but have seen only hundreds of miles. I have been over clouds, between two layers, or actually in the formation, for hours on end, and have seen no ships excepting very near land. However, on the Pacific flight I took along a chart showing the position of every ship on the course that night. The possibility of one little airplane and one little ship passing near enough to see each other in that rather large ocean seemed ridiculous.

I had been flying off the islands for about six hours when I became aware of a pink light to my right—pink in contrast to the stars. I realized I was actually seeing a ship. I couldn't see it as a ship, of course. It appeared only as a revolving pinkish light.

All the vessels had agreed to keep their searchlights on in case I was anywhere around. I flashed my landing lights, which are pretty bright, three times. Then again, until I got an answering signal from that little thing 8,000 feet below. I was tuned in on KFI in Los Angeles. Whatever the program was, suddenly it was blocked out by code crackling like buckshot in my ears and I knew that ship was sending word to shore it had sighted me overhead. At that time I was nine hundred miles on my course, as correctly as could be.

After this friendly exchange with the ship, the clouds came together below me, blocking all sight of water. Meanwhile I could see the tops of those clouds and as I looked ahead the stars around the horizon were dim. It was as if a veil hung between me and them. The veil crept higher and higher up the horizon until it enveloped my plane and I could see nothing outside of the cockpit. Fine rain-drops were on the glass and as suddenly as I had gotten into the rain squall, for such it was, I came out again into the moonlight and starlight.

I continued to run through little rain squalls for possibly two hours. At no time during the flight did the outside temperature register below forty degrees. However, I had the cockpit window open a bit and the cold rain beat in on me until I became thoroughly chilled. I thought it would be rather pleasant to have a cup of hot chocolate. So I did, and it was. Indeed that was the most interesting cup of chocolate I have ever had, sitting up eight thousand feet over the middle of the Pacific Ocean, quite alone.

After midnight the moon set and I was alone with the stars. I have often said that the lure of flying is the lure of beauty, and I need no other flight to convince me that the reason flyers fly, whether they know it or not, is the esthetic appeal of flying.

On the Atlantic trip I thought the most beautiful thing I should ever see would be dawn over the ocean. But then I did not see dawn as it was obstructed by clouds. This time I was more fortunate. A shadow of light played around the horizon and suddenly the stars were gone. Dawn is a fearful thing to see from the air. Only by wearing dark glasses can a pilot face the rising sun for any length of time because of the brilliance of the light.

In addition to enjoying its beauty, that dawn over the Pacific was disconcerting. For the sun made its appearance well to the right of the course I was following. It seemed to me I should be flying much more in its direction than I was. For a brief moment I wondered if all night long I had been headed for Alaska! I checked my charts and I checked my compass and everything seemed to be as it should—so I could only conclude that the sun was wrong and I was right!

After it became light enough to see, I found myself over a closely packed white cloud bank, which seemed to extend to the ends of the earth and looked extraordinarily like stiffly beaten whites of eggs. I don't know if there is anything in the power of suggestion, but about that time I ate a hard-boiled egg, the only solid food I had during the flight.

My radio frequency was not particularly efficient after sun-up. However, I kept on broadcasting periodically, knowing that listening shore stations would at least get my signal and thus know I was still afloat. Being fairly sure they could understand little of what I said, I became slightly careless with words. I commented on the scenery, which wasn't much, and made other remarks. After flying over this monotonous fog—you have no idea how wearying it can be—for one hour, for two hours, for three hours, I remember saying into my little hand microphone: "I am getting tired of this fog." My message was picked up "I'm getting tired." So a nurse and physician were dispatched to the airport at Oakland to revive the exhausted flyer when and if she arrived. Of course I wasn't tired at all. No one should undertake a long flight who becomes fatigued after staying up just one night under normal flying conditions.

About the fifteenth hour out the fog bank began to break up (as it often does near land) and holes appeared through which I could look down and see the water once again. This time it was blue in the morning sun, ruffled with little crinkles. I glanced casually down through a cloud window and there was another boat. I cocked the wing of my plane up and went down through that hole faster, I think, than I ever flew before, from 8,000 feet to two hundred. A large dollar sign on the steamer funnel established it as the Dollar Liner *President Pierce* coming from San Francisco. It was going in the right direction, too, and just where it should be, according to my chart. And so was I.

I circled the ship several times, wanting the Captain to be sure to notice me. Then I lined myself up with the wake of the vessel, which I could see for more than a mile behind it, and found that the course I had been flying coincided exactly with the track made by the ship, which was a very good check on direction. I could not talk directly with the steamer, so I radioed San Francisco asking for its position and within fifteen minutes received word that I was then three hundred miles off the coast of California, exactly on my course.

There is no doubt that the last hour of any flight is the hardest. If there are any clouds about to make shadows one is likely to see much imaginary land. I saw considerable territory in the Pacific which California should annex!

When I actually first sighted land I was flying about 1,800 feet off the surface of the water, considerably below the summits of the coastal hills. As I approached shore I strained my eyes to see something recognizable, and there was nothing. However, I noticed a low place in the hills, and I thought, like the bear, I would go over the mountains to see what I could see.

Drawing nearer, I pulled the nose of the plane up, eagerly peering ahead as we floated gently over those hospitable hills. And there lay San Francisco Bay in front of me. All I had to do was to go across and sit down.

The landing at Oakland contrasted with that in Ireland in 1932. Near Londonderry, after scaring most of the cows in the neighborhood, I pulled up in a farmer's back yard. Three people came out to see what was in the airplane. I pushed the hatch back and stuck out my head. Not knowing the proper phrase for the situation I simply said, "I'm from America." It made no impression whatsoever on the reception committee.

At Oakland I did not have to explain whence I came.

Mexican Flight

There were three factors which determined me to try a flight to Mexico. One, I had a plane in perfect condition for a long distance effort. Two, I had been officially invited by the Mexican Government. (I had never been invited before. I just went to Ireland.) Three, Wiley Post.

I remember telling Wiley Post of my plans. He walked across the room, looked at a globe standing on the table, and asked me what route I intended to use from Mexico City to New York. I told him I planned to fly in as straight a line as possible.

"Are you cutting across the Gulf?" he asked.

I said I was. He measured it with his fingers.

"That's about 700 miles. Almost half an Atlantic. How much time do you lose if you go around by the shore?"

I told him I saved probably one hour, or a little more, by following the straight line.

Wiley said: "Amelia, don't do it. It's too dangerous."

I couldn't believe my ears. Did Wiley Post, the man who had braved every sort of hazard in his stratosphere flying, really regard a simple little flight from Mexico City to New York across the Gulf as too hazardous? If so, I could scarcely wait to be on my way.

On April 19, 1935, NR 965Y (my Vega) and I started from Burbank, California, for Mexico City. Slightly over thirteen hours later we landed at Valbuena Airport, 1,700 miles southward.

From a pilot's standpoint that was an interesting journey. The start made before midnight was lit by a generous moon which gilded the hills gloriously, but by the time I had reached the arid stretches of the Gulf of California there crept up a white haze which made it difficult to tell what was water and what was sand ahead. Only when I could catch a glimpse of the moonlight on the water or see the black shadows of crinkled sand directly below, could I tell which was which. Even the mechanical difficulties which beset the early hours of the flight—chiefly an engine which overheated because of a faulty propeller setting—could not mar the rare loveliness of the night and of the far-flung countryside which slumbered beneath.

Slightly below Mazatlán, on the Mexican coast, a thousand miles or so from the starting point, the chart directed me to turn easterly toward Mexico City, six hundred miles away. Here were ruffles of mountains sloping upward into the high tableland of central Mexico. I was flying by compass and successfully located the towns of Tepic and Guadalajara, and thought perhaps I would escape the fate that had been promised me, that of straying on the final stretch of the journey. But I suddenly realized there was a railroad beneath me which had no business being where it was if I were where I ought to be.

I was flying at an altitude of more than 10,000 feet, with mountains and plains not far below me. I had counted on arriving before one o'clock Mexican time, but when that hour came I realized that, while probably near my destination, my exact location was uncertain.

Just about then an insect, or possibly some infinitesimal speck of dirt, lodged in my eye. In addition to being extremely painful, that minute accident played havoc with my sight. So, with the maps, such as they were, blurred even to my "good eye," which at once went on strike in sympathy with its ailing mate, and having the feeling of being lost anyway, I decided to sit down and ask the way.

My landing place was a pasture not unreminiscent of another landing in Ireland, although here the cattle were stolidly indifferent to my arrival while their transAtlantic brethren (sistern?) raised a temperamental ruckus when my roaring motor disturbed their privacy. This field was decorated not with shamrock but by occasional cactus and prickly pear. The near-by village, I found, was named Nopala, which means prickly pear.

No sooner was I down, after brushing the field a couple of times to see if a landing was possible, than cowboys and villagers sprang up miraculously. They were helpful, polite and not at all astonished, even when their visitor turned out to be feminine. My pasture was a dry lake-bed, not overly large, but level and reasonably free from dangerous obstructions. My Spanish does not exist, and none of the vaqueros spoke English. So our negotiations were mostly accomplished with signs and smiles, which sufficed well enough, particularly with a bright dark-skinned boy who established my location on the map, which turned out to be about fifty miles from Mexico City.

After taxiing the ship to the end of the clear space, a couple of the more enthusiastic spectators rode to the middle of my "runway," confident they would be helpful there. To make it quite clear that such a location would be thoroughly unfortunate when my ship charged down on them for the take-off, it was necessary to climb out of the cockpit and plow afoot through the dust for further discussion. Once the point was well established, my friends withdrew to the sidelines and saw to it that the cattle, goats and children were herded to safety.

Actually there was not much difficulty in getting into the air again, and half an hour later I was given a more official welcome at the Capital.

The ensuing days were a kaleidoscope of things done and seen, and hospitable people met. "Fun in Mexico" would be an appropriate title. President Lazaro Cardenas graciously extended official greetings and privileges. We barged through the flower-laden floating gardens of Xochimilco, a bucolic tropic Venice on the fringe of the Capital. We saw the Basque game, jai alai, a fast and furious glorified squash; and a charro fiesta, which is to say a cowboy exhibition, demonstrating that superb horsemanship is the same art the world over, needing, like music, no interpretation.

Unfortunately opportunity lacked to discuss with women, as I would have liked to, their strivings and ambitions. What law and tradition permit them to do outside the home I am uncertain. While I met only sheltered women among the well-to-do, I saw many worn with the hard labor of farm life, and briefly touched a few groups of self-supporting city women workers. I saw enough of the spirit of the new Mexico, however, to want to know more of what reforms the new order holds for its women. I, for one, hope for the day when women will know no restrictions because of sex but will be individuals free to live their lives as men are free—irrespective of the continent or country where they happen to live.

At a concert given in my honor I admired the cowboy regalia worn by the musicians. Forthwith, to my embarrassment (and pleasure!) I found that Secretary of State Portes Gil had ordained that I should have such a one for myself. This outfit is as traditional as the pink coat of the British huntsman or the kilts of the Highlander. Mine, as delivered some days later, is a formal creation of blue and silver, topped by a picturesque sombrero, heavy with corresponding trimmings. How such a colorful costume may be adapted to flying is a sartorial problem I never mastered.

Mine, alas, was a flying visit in both senses of the word. Scarcely had I alighted when the problems of departing pressed upon us.

In Mexico City both the military and civilian airports are excellent. But at the mile-and-a-half altitude their runways, while ample for normal flying, were not as long as my overloaded plane required. So we explored the mud-caked flats which once had been the bottom of Lake Texcoco adjoining the metropolis and there on the lake-bed, aided by Mexican soldiers, who filled a ditch and shaved off hummocks, we contrived a home-made airport with a runway three miles in length.

I have often said the most potent letters in the alphabet of aviation are "w" and "p." In flyers' shorthand "wp" means "weather permitting." It's a wise pilot who prefaces announcement of his plans with that proviso.

For eight days in Mexico City "w" had not "p." Not until one o'clock in the morning of May ninth did I learn definitely that the elements had relented. Over the telephone from the Weather Bureau in New York Mr. Putnam gave me the final reports as prepared by our old friend Dr. James H. Kimball, dean of record flights.

So I sent word out to the men at the plane to fill the tanks with the 470 gallons of gasoline required, while I curled up for a few hours' sleep. Then at four o'clock, Edmundo Rendon, our able interpreter, drove me to the home-made runway, staked out with flags for my guidance.

Earlier in the day Charles Baughan, a veteran Lockheed pilot who operates a sky-taxi service in Mexico City, had flown my plane from the Pan American hangar over to the level stretches of the lake-bed, whence the take-off was planned. The drums of gasoline already were there, with soldiers, under the direction of Captain Casolando, to guard them and the plane, and to herd people, cows, horses and goats out of harm's way.

Under the direction of Baughan the "gassing up" was accomplished, while Casasolo, Pan American star mechanic, gave my Wasp motor its final check by the light of automobile headlights meagerly supplemented with the dim radiance of a very young moon.

That day I had breakfast in Mexico City and supper in New York—a very early breakfast, to be sure, and a decidedly late supper, for it was 10:30 when I landed at Newark, 2,185 miles to the north.

It was a few minutes past six, Mexican time, when I took off. Although I used perhaps a full mile of the improvised runway the plane got into the air with surprising ease. My Vega was always doing that—surprising me with superb performance. Dire predictions had been made regarding that overload take-off in the rare air of an 8,000 foot altitude. But all I had to do was to keep the plane moving in a straight line and hold it on the ground until we'd built up a speed well over a hundred miles an hour—then it just flew itself into the air.

Slowly I climbed to 10,000 feet, to skim over the mountains that hem in the high central valley where the city lies, separating it from the lands that slope down to the sea. Majestic Popocatepetl raised its snowy head to the south, luminous in the rays of the rising sun. A fairyland of beauty lay below and about me—so lovely as almost to distract a pilot's attention from the task at hand, that of herding a heavy plane out of that great upland saucer and over the mountains that make its rim.

Seen from the air, all countries have characteristics peculiar to themselves. Ireland is recognizable by its green fields, white cottages, and thatched roofs. Like the ubiquitous baseball diamond of the United States, most Mexican towns have their unmistakable bull-ring sitting in the midst of adobe houses and walled gardens. These were vivid in my visual memories of that morning's flight.

Once across the divide, clouds banked continuously below me, stretching down over the Gulf. I saw little but their fleecy contours with the exception of one brief glimpse of a group of oil tanks which I estimated to be close to Tampico. Thence I bore northeasterly in a straight line across the Gulf for New Orleans, a distance of about 700 miles. From New Orleans on, radio communication between my plane and airway stations below was constant. Indeed, our conversations were so continuous I felt as if I were more-or-less sliding home along a neighborly "party line."

All in all, the flight was marked by a delightful precision. Everything worked as it should. Its only exciting moments followed my landing at Newark when the crowd overflowed the field. In due course I was rescued from my plane by husky policemen, one of whom in the ensuing melee took possession of my right arm and another of my left leg. Their plan was to get me to the shelter of a near-by police car, but with the best of intentions their execution lacked co-ordination. For the arm-holder started to go one way while he who clasped my leg set out in the opposite direction. The result provided the victim with a fleeting taste of the tortures of the rack. But, at that, it was fine to be home again.

Preparation

To begin, I should describe how the world flight project developed. I have already told that the fond idea of acquiring a multi-motored plane first took form when I was flying over the Gulf of Mexico.

After being just a passenger over the Atlantic in 1928, I wanted to duplicate the crossing alone in my own plane. I pursued the dream of a solo flight for four years before it became a reality in 1932. One ocean led naturally to another and two years later, through hard work and generous help, the opportunity came to try the Pacific. After that crossing from Honolulu to Oakland I thought of a hundred things I could do with a new plane. I was so full of ideas that they spilt over and my husband had to listen to my burbling by the hour. Not only did I want to make a longer flight than any I had attempted before, but I wanted to test some human reactions to flying. Of myself, and others as I found them, I planned to make human guinea pigs.

The aviation industry has been so busy with mechanical and economic problems that the effects of flying on personnel have not always been given the attention they deserve. I am interested in finding out whether one kind of food is better than another during flight; i.e., the effects of altitude on metabolism. Also I should like to know the rate at which fatigue is induced by the myriad instruments a modern pilot must use. What will stratosphere flying do to creatures accustomed to the dense air of lower altitudes? Are men and women different in their reactions to air travel? If so, how? And perhaps, why?

With the modern plane it seems to me that too often in the attainment of speed other considerations have been sacrificed. Safety, especially. Perhaps we would do well to go back to the elementary flying-machines of the early days and work forward from them all over again.

The existing standards of speed, size and luxury cannot practically be abandoned, now that the air-traveling public has become accustomed to them. But rather than focusing on the problem of making tomorrow's planes bigger and faster, I, for one, would like to see the technical genius of present-day aviation—and the industry possesses extraordinary genius—develop a plane that actually could stay in the air while moving perhaps only forty miles an hour, and one that in a pinch could land at thirty. Which, I think, can come without sacrificing top speeds, size or comfort.

Many flyers feel the modern plane has become too complex. In the cockpit of my own Electra, for instance, there are over a hundred dials and gadgets which I either have to look at or twiddle. The pilot's prayer, I am sure, is not for more cunning and specialized instruments, but for a simplification of those existing. However, these are but the opinions of one flyer who finds herself particularly interested in the human aspects of the machine, as it affects those using it.

For a couple of years I had been pleasantly associated with Purdue University of Lafayette, Indiana, as a periodic and rather peripatetic faculty member. Purdue is a forward-looking institution building an important aviation department. It is one of the few universities in the world that has its own landing field.

Additionally, it is co-educational. Of its 6,000 students approximately 1,000 are women. The problems and opportunities of these girls were quite as much my concern as aviation matters. Perhaps I have something of a chip on my shoulder when it comes to modern feminine education. Often youngsters are sadly miscast. I have known girls who should be tinkering with mechanical things instead of making dresses, and boys who would do better at cooking than engineering.

One of my favorite phobias is that girls, especially those whose tastes aren't routine, often don't get a fair break. The situation is not new. It has come down through the generations, an inheritance of age-old customs which produced the corollary that women are bred to timidity.

The mechanical-minded boy may have a field-day from the time his legs are long enough to toddle down to the corner garage. For all anyone cares, he may be weaned on piston rings and carburetors, and may remain beautifully grimy for indefinite periods. But with his sister it is different. With rare exceptions, the delights of finding out what makes a motor go, or batting the bumps out of a bent fender, are joys reserved for masculinity.

The girl who wants to do that sort of thing has such a hard time finding a place to do it that for long I have harbored a very special pet ambition. Among my other somewhat suppressed desires it is classified under the letter "T." The imaginary file card reads, "Tinkering: For Girls Only." The plan is to endow a catch-as-catch-can machine-shop, where girls may tinker to their heart's content with motors, lathes, jigsaws, gadgets, and diverse hickies of their own creation. Where they may sprawl on their back, peering up into the innards of engines, and likely as not get oil in their hair. Where they can make things and have the fun of finding out how things are made, why engines perk, clocks tick, radios yowl, and something of the every-day mechanical marvels which—given the chance—many of them would master quite as well as Brother Bill. And emerge somewhere in the scale between grease-monkeys and inventors. Or, negatively, with at least their lack of aptitude revealed.

All of which is a considerable digression in an account which is supposed to deal with my world-circling project. The subjects, however, are related.

The flight was to be the forerunner of activities at Purdue, where, miraculously, there exists a real comprehension of the quaint view-point I have tried to indicate. Practical mechanical training, engineering and the like, is available without discouragement to women students there. An alluring field was opened in our discussions of a course to be designed in "household engineering." Many a stay-at-home girl would welcome practical training in what to do when the door-bell fails to function, the plumbing clogs, the gas-range leaks, the fuse blows out, the windmill pump goes haywire, and the thousand-and-one other mechanical indispositions that can occur about the house, often easily enough fixed if one has rudimentary knowledge how to fix them.

Which, perhaps, explains my enthusiasm for Purdue, womanwise as well as aviation-wise.

One day last summer President Edward C. Elliott of Purdue asked my husband what most interested me beyond immediate academic matters. Mr. Putnam, a practicing believer in wives doing what they do best, is an approving and helpful partner in all my projects. So he divulged my suppressed pilot's yearning for a bigger and better airplane. Not only to go to far places further and faster and more safely, but essentially for pioneering in aviation education and technical experimentation.

So, in due time, I came into possession of my two-motor Lockheed Electra. Its purchase was made possible chiefly through the Purdue Research Foundation, aided by such friends as J. K. Lilly, Vincent Bendix, and others, mostly within the aviation industry, and by the generosity of manufacturers who seemed to feel that my activities were helpful in promoting aviation, and especially, perhaps, in overcoming women's "sales resistance" to air travel.

I had intended to undertake a year's research with my plane and thereafter plan some interesting flight. But circumstances made it appear wiser to postpone the research and attempt the flight first.

My "flying laboratory" became equipped with all that is modern in instruments. It has a Sperry Gyro-Pilot, an automatic device which actually flies the ship unaided. There is a Bendix radio direction finder which points the way to any selected broadcasting station within its range. There is the finest two-way voice and code Western Electric communication equipment in whose installation the Bell Laboratories, under the aegis of Dr. Frank B. Jewett, co-operated.

The plane itself is a two-motor, all-metal monoplane, with retractable landing gear. It is a big brother to the two Lockhead Vegas which I have used on previous flights. It has a normal cruising speed of about 180 miles an hour and a top speed in excess of 200. With the special gasoline tanks that have been installed in the fuselage, capable of carrying 1,150 gallons, it has a cruising radius in excess of 4,000 miles. With full load the ship weighs about 15,000 pounds. It is powered with two Wasp "H" engines, developing 1100 horsepower.

Anticipation, I suppose, sometimes exceeds realization. Whatever the final outcome of the trip itself, certainly there was extraordinary interest in the months of planning for it.

Preparation, I have often said, is rightly two-thirds of any venture.

Preparation for the world flight occupied many months. There were the mechanical problems of the ship and its operation and far-flung arrangements for the journey.

When you plan an automobile journey through New England, or, say, to Yellowstone, the needed maps can be had at any filling station. But with a flight around the world, much of it off the beaten paths of established air transport, there are complexities. It took many weeks to get all the maps and charts we wanted. Once secured, the courses to be followed were laid out in detail on them, mostly by Commander Clarence Williams of Los Angeles, who had helped me plot previous flights.

In final form flight charts are really lovely things. On them are drawn the compass courses with their periodic changes, distances, airports and the like. As supplementary data accumulates the marginal notes assume encyclopedic proportions. They concern details about airports, service facilities, prevailing winds, characteristics of local weather and terrain, critical altitudes, emergency landing possibilities and the like.

In assembling the precious data a tower of helpfulness was Jacques de Sibour, an old friend of ours who, with his wife Violette (both pilots), is intimately familiar with flying conditions in much of the most difficult territory involved.

All important in our budding campaign were the arrangements for fuel and service. As our plans progressed the world-wide organization of the Standard Oil Company of New Jersey and its associates co-operated in assembling information and in "spotting" fuel supplies at designated points. At certain fields scattered here and there, competent mechanics were provided for and spare parts assembled.

Living with those maps and charts was absorbing and instructive. My knowledge of geography—at least theoretically—increased from week to week. To sit in the sunshine of the lanai in my California home, tracking monsoons to their lairs and appraising rainfalls in India and take-off conditions at African airports, was an adventure in itself. Some day I would like to write a piece about the fun of voyaging with maps—without ever leaving home.

The proposed route, as originally laid out, was from Oakland to Honolulu, thence to Port Darwin in Northern Australia, via New

Guinea and a tiny pin-point of an island called Howland, half a degree north of the equator about 1,800 miles southwest of Hawaii. That was part one. Part two, a lengthier stretch over fabulous lands, extended from Australia to the west coast of Africa by way of Arabia. The third section was the South Atlantic. The fourth from Brazil north. I felt that if I could do any one of these creditably I should not be disappointed.

While on previous flights I had always been alone, this time I planned to take a navigator with me.

In three hops the Electra and I had to cross more than 6,500 miles of water, two of them broken by no land whatever, and all the way with no intermediate landing fields. It did not seem good sense to try such a crossing without the aid of celestial navigation. On two previous ocean flights and from Mexico across the Gulf I've "dead reckoned" and made my landfall. But then I was aiming at continents, not small spots of land in the mightiest ocean. Hawaii, 2,400 miles from California, would be hard to find by this method alone. Howland Island—dimensions, less than a mile by two miles—1,800 miles further on, would be a fantastically tiny target. To take every precaution to find it, I had four means. One, dead reckoning (which is simply the estimate of position based on speed in a given direction maintained for a definite time); two, radio bearings from ships at sea and shore stations; three, a radio direction finder in my cockpit; four, celestial navigation. So far as my experience goes I believe a lone pilot cannot take an accurate sight at will, airplanes being the complicated mechanisms they are today. So I asked Captain Harry Manning to be navigator.

My first meeting with Captain Manning was when he was skipper of the United States liner *Roosevelt*, on which I returned after my first flight across the Atlantic in 1928. On that trip he talked navigation to me. We agreed that some day, when the chance came, we would team up on a flight. Now, eight years later, he still wanted to ship on such an aerial voyage and I still wanted him to.

The plane had been fitted with special windows for his work. He had a good-sized table to hold necessary charts. Chronometers were beside the table, shock-mounted on rubber. Other "chart-room" equipment included altimeter, air-speed and drift indicators, pelorus and compass. The navigator had access to any part of the plane, for a catwalk over the large gasoline tanks connected the cabin in the rear with the cockpit.

There, briefly, is the Foreword to the flight. Enacting it occupied me (and many others) through last winter. By March we were approaching the goal of departure.

To a large degree I had been able to launch previous flights without discussing them in advance. In aviation, talking before one has anything to talk about is unusually poor policy. So many things can happen before the take-off to change the plan of action, or even cause complete abandonment of the adventure, that most pilots prefer to play owl and say nothing. However, in this case that wasn't possible, one result being that for many months I was privileged to answer many questions—if I could.

"*Why* are you attempting this around-the-world flight?" Such was one of the most pertinent queries, whose answer may as well be recorded here.

"Because I want to." That was as near a complete reply as I could devise. Here was shining adventure, beckoning with new experiences, added knowledge of flying, of peoples—of myself. I felt that with the flight behind me I would be more useful to me and to the program we had planned at Purdue.

Then, too, there was my belief that now and then women should do for themselves what men have already done—and occasionally what men have not done—thereby establishing themselves as persons, and perhaps encouraging other women toward greater independence of thought and action. Some such consideration was a contributing reason for my wanting to do what I so much wanted to do.

Honolulu Flight

About half past four on the afternoon of March 17 we took off from Oakland, bound for Honolulu.

The "we" of this departure was a crew four times more sizeable than I had ever embarked with before. Beside myself, there was Harry Manning, Fred Noonan, and Paul Mantz. I planned to drop Mantz at Honolulu, Noonan at Howland, and Manning in Australia. At the time we said here would be an occasion where it would be the males who'd do the walking home! But the best laid plans of mice and pilots can go awry, and so awry went mine that all four of us returned together from the islands by steamer. But before getting to that, let me set down the story of the flight itself.

Fred Noonan, tops among aerial navigators, was a veteran of a dozen Pacific air crossings for Pan American, who signed on to co-operate with Harry Manning on the first two difficult over-water hops. Appropriate to the day, which was St. Patrick's, and the forebears the name Noonan implied, he wore a shamrock.

At the last minute Paul Mantz decided he would like to hitch-hike to Honolulu. I was glad to have him, for his presence meant not only a relief pilot on the way over, but the benefit of his technical skill in checking the ship before the long jump to Howland. Parenthetically, it was only after I had agreed to take him that I awoke to the fact that I was unwittingly playing the role of understudy to Cupid. For Paul confessed that the big reason he wanted to go to Honolulu just then wasn't solely his professional devotion to my project, but the fact that his fiancée, Mrs. Theresa Miner,* was already at sea on the

*Paul and "Terry" were married in Burbank on August 19, 1937.

31

Matson Line steamer *Malolo*, Hawaii-bound. It seemed the quickest way for him to rejoin her was to fly with me.

For a week intermittent rain held us at Oakland. On the day of our departure more rain fell and from lowering clouds some final showers descended even while the ship was being gassed. But by four o'clock the sun shone through gray cloud-banks to the westward, gilding the Golden Gate with good omen.

With 947 gallons of gasoline on board, the Electra had a heavy load to raise from the wet field. Paul Mantz and I had carefully worked out the piloting technique of that start. It was a team-play take-off—each with his job, I at the controls, Paul handling throttles and retractable landing gear. The 1100 horses of my two Wasp engines leaped so gallantly to the task of lifting 14,000 pounds into the sky that our wheels left the ground after the almost unbelievably short run of 1,897 feet—as subsequent measurement showed. Incidentally, special one hundred octane gasoline gave the motors extra power.

Once aloft, I throttled down. Engines have human attributes—they usually respond to kindly treatment. With a long grind before them I wished to give mine the least possible punishment.

The first few hours of flight are often indicative of what is to come, mechanically. Therefore, I wanted daylight for a while in order to be able to watch more easily plane and engine reactions. Further, a sharp horizon line is an aid to pilots; whether they are conscious of it or not, in keeping an overloaded plane on even keel.

As we passed through it, the Golden Gate was truly golden. Behind us dark clouds closed in. But westward the sky was cheerful with late afternoon sunlight, which burnished the slopes of Mount Tamalpais on one hand and story-book San Francisco on the other, as we headed westward over the great new bridge, a thread of steel below us, specked with crawling tiny beetles that were automobiles homeward bound.

An hour out from Alameda we sighted Pan American's Clipper, silhouetted against a towering bank of cumulus, sun-flecked clouds. We flew near enough actually to obtain a photograph. This was the first time I had seen another plane at sea, and later I learned that in all their Pacific crossings up to then Pan American ships had never sighted each other. For Ed Musick, pilot on this Clipper, this was a "first" too. Shortly, with our greater speed, we slowly left the big flying boat astern. All of us, I am sure, were impressed with the unusualness of meeting, and then leaving, another plane out there over the lonely stretches of the ocean. Unusual as such an occurrence is today, before long it doubtless will be as commonplace as passing transports on our continental airways.

Here are verbatim extracts from my log book as they were penciled in it that night over the Pacific:

Clipper ship   2 photographs.
1:15   rainbow
1:30   ship

Ice in carb. Rt engine in and out.
Leaned too much. Then rainbow.

Golden edged clouds ahead, then the golden nothingness of sunset beyond. I am glad we started with as much daylight as we did. Some of the squalls we have come through would have been less pleasant at night.

Paul and I have some cocoa 3 hrs. out. There is still a glow in the west. I have been flying most of the time. Now Paul does and I watch instruments. Stars about. The navigators are working like mad. Harry has just had a long radio discourse.

The aft cabin is lighted with a weird green blue light. Our instruments show pink.

The sky rose yellow.

The night has come. It is eleven o'clock. Cal. time. The sea is lovely. Venus is setting ahead and to the right. The moon is a lifesaver. It gives us a horizon to fly by. It shines on the engine cowls and into the cockpit.

We have much the same formation as on my flight. Fluffy clouds, tho more open sea.

6–7 hours out. The stars are brilliant but with the moon they cant be seen on horizon. Harry comes up to work the radio. Paul flies while Harry works over my head.

6:35   Harry reports we're ahead of the dead reckoning. Noonan is just figuring position. Gas so far is o.k.

The ship now flies like an airplane with almost 2000 lbs rt up.

180 mph Boy oh Boy I hope the navigators know what they're talking about.

KFI just reported at 12:15 PST Weather report from Steamer Monterey. Also W. T. Miller. Paul called Burbank on 3105.

Noonan asks to hold her steady while he takes string of sights. Pan Am in Oa Pan Am says to contact Honolulu now 1 A.M.

Harry has just talked with Hon. The moon has sunk into a bed of clouds. We are now using the Sperry to save our eyes as there is practically no horizon. Just the type of cloud formation and lack of vis. I had last time, only then I had no Sperry. little helper.

Clouds are getting fuzzy I think. For a while they were like mere firm white dumplings just under our wings. Then they ran down hill and lay swallowed in the moonlight several thousand feet below. Now they are more formless. However stars still above.

The navigators are having coffee. I smell it.

The night is clearer now. The clouds are white with dark islands—where the sea shows through.

It is now 4:10 PST. We have been flying over a stretch of open sea so the sky looks light. Now we reach some clouds with holes in them. Now and then a star seems to rise from one of these holes. Curious illusion.

The sky certainly seems lighter. But its too early for dawn. I have just eaten an apple. Paul a tomato because there wasn't any for him.

This was the first time since the Friendship Flight in 1928 that I'd had company when voyaging over an ocean. Not that there were any particularly social aspects about this experience. In the cockpit we pilots were too constantly busy for much conversation, while the navigators were equally occupied in their fuselage chart-room aft of the extra fuel tanks, which in my Electra occupy much of the space normally used by passengers. There they had the tools of their exacting trade—the business of finding where one may be, from the stars, the sun and dead reckoning, aided by such devices as sextants, octants, chronometers and drift indicator.

Communication between our pilot's cockpit and the navigators in their cubbyhole was carried on by means of a cut-down bamboo fishpole, with an office clip at the end to hold the cards upon which messages were written. Most interesting information came up to the pilots from the "navigation department." Not only was it important to know our position at a given moment, but our rate of speed and the computation of fuel consumption and quantity remaining in the tanks. Incidentally, we arrived at Hawaii with more than four hours' supply of gasoline remaining, which would have given us over 600 miles of additional flying, a satisfactory safety margin.

Compared with the Atlantic flights, made without benefit of radio, this venture seemed almost chatty and neighborly. Constantly we were in touch with the world, almost surfeited with the programs on which we could tune in, not to mention the messages broadcast for our special benefit, and the periodic reports of our position and progress we sent out. All of us were so occupied throughout the night there was no time to doze, even had there been inclination. Indeed, there was hardly opportunity to eat. We carried box lunches, but I noticed upon arrival very few sandwiches were missing. I ate one sandwich myself and an apple. The others satisfied themselves with hot chocolate and coffee, snatched in paper cups from the thermos bottles.

Fred Noonan's navigation proved all one could expect. Throughout the night the stars told him (via his bubble octant) where we were, while Harry Manning worked the radio.

At one point, when we were a couple of hundred miles from Hawaii, Fred told me to drop down through the clouds and steer a certain course.

"Keep the Makapuu beacon ten degrees on the starboard bow," he ordered.

What he meant was that I should tune my Bendix radio direction finder to indicate the location of the beacon, and then head the plane as he directed. This was the first time I had used this recently

Daylight—
comes atlant—
the stars fade
mean throttled down
to 120 indicated airspeed
so not—to arrive in
darkness   we are
burning less than
20 gals of gas at 1000 ft
the have turned on our
Makapu.   Keep with 10
degrees to starboard bow
is the order

Page of log book kept on first world flight take-off from Oakland to Honolulu.

developed Bendix instrument. On this Pacific hop it was one of the most interesting and valuable on board, performing perfectly.

Here are some further extracts from my flight diary:

> Daylight comes at last. The stars fade. We are throttled down to 120 indicated airspeed so not to arrive in darkness. We are burning less than 20 gals. of gas at 10000 ft. We have tuned in on Makapu. Keep it 10 degrees to starboard bow is the order.
>
> The generator just went out. Harry has held the key down so long it grew tired. Whats a gen. if he got his bearings? We cant see yet what we're over. It might be desert. Looking back the silhouetted clouds might be hills (rolling) against the twilight sky and now and then we pass over a "lake."
>
> 80 miles from Makapu. Fred says start down.

At 5:40 in the morning, Honolulu time, we sighted Diamond Head, that friendly landmark which I had last seen on January 11, 1935, when at dusk on a cloudy afternoon my heavily laden Lockheed Vega headed eastward bound for the California coast. It put in an appearance through the morning mists exactly where and when Fred expected it, which was most comforting.

Making the landfall that morning was even pleasanter than my first view of California's shore line two years ago. After all, it would require ingenuity to miss a continent, which I was aiming for then. Hawaii, however, is something else again and we all knew how easily it could be passed by.

I felt I owed an apology to the people who rose early to greet us when we landed at Wheeler Field. Perhaps I should have been more considerate and tried to arrange the arrival at a later hour. But that was difficult, because it was so desirable to time the departure from Oakland in daylight. Having visited those lovely islands before, I was accustomed to the very special hospitality of Hawaii, but I did not expect so many of its friendly people to go without breakfast that they might welcome us. And speaking of breakfast, a bright particular memory of the immediate aftermaths of our arrival were the so-fresh scrambled eggs miraculously awaiting us at the home of Colonel and Mrs. John McDonnell.

We had hoped to push on to Howland promptly but soon found that weather conditions to the southwestward weren't what they might be. Delay was evidently inevitable. But if one has to wait, in all the world there is no pleasanter place to do the waiting than in Honolulu. Again, as before on my 1935 Pacific solo, I was ensconced in the lovely Waikiki beach home of Mr. and Mrs. Chris Holmes. Six hours of sleep there, topped off by luxurious sun-bathing on the lanai, whence one may regard the tropic scene through the rippling fronds of cocoanut palms, banished all traces of fatigue. Meals appeared wherever and whenever one awoke, while the quantities of pineapple juice I consumed between times were fabulous.

Back at the field Wilbur Thomas, Pratt & Whitney's representative in Hawaii, was on his toes to get at the Wasp engines. I told him he was one of the very few men in the world I would let touch them before the time rolled around for their regular overhaul, many hours away. Beautiful motors, you know, are sometimes best left alone when they are functioning perfectly. However mine, under the best possible direction, forthwith received appropriate mechanical rub-down and massage, so to speak, just to keep them in the pink of condition.

In passing, I do want to record some "thank yous" among the many due those who were kind to me. Army and Navy officers and men all contributed their utmost, my gratitude going particularly to General Barton K. Young, Colonel John McDonnell, and Major Samuel Grierson. Two civilian accomplices of my previous visit, "Bill" Cogswell and Nat Farbman—island representatives of our good friend Sydney Bowman of San Francisco—were helpfully on hand always. There are so many! Richard B. Black, and all the personnel of the *Itasca,* with their fruitless waiting at Howland; Bill Miller of the Department of Commerce, Lieutenant Frank Johnson of the Coast Guard, Bob Oertel of Standard Oil, women friends like Benigna Green and Bess Young at Honolulu. And especially the mechanics and technicians who labored in and out of hours at Burbank, Oakland, Honolulu, and elsewhere. To them I owe so much. Some day I hope to shake their hands and have them know I realize what a helpless part of any flight a pilot, without them, would be.

Our time—15 hours and 47 minutes from Oakland to Honolulu—

had established a record for the east-west crossing. That is an interesting commentary on the progress of flying equipment, particularly as concerns speed. Actually, we were going about as slowly as possible. We throttled back the engines and most of the way our craft was "under wraps." For once, tail winds were almost an embarrassment: so far as concerns speed, it would have been easier to go faster. The Electra, or similar craft, can comfortably cut a couple of hours off the left-handed record we set up 'most any time under favoring conditions.

From Honolulu I wrote on March 19: "The element of speed is far from uppermost in such a flight as this. It can't be. Quite truly, I'm in no hurry. It was disappointing yesterday that bad weather prevented us carrying on. But doubtless similar delays will occur later. My ambition is no time mark. There is no 'record' to shoot at. That will come for others later. We'll see globe-girdling flights whose brevity will take your breath away. As for this present venture, I just want to progress as safely and sanely as day-to-day conditions make possible, give myself and the Electra the experience of seeing what we can of this very interesting world at its waistline, and, with good fortune, get back with plane and pilot all "in one piece.' "

Seemingly I spoke out of turn, for the next morning my poor plane was anything but "in one piece." Badly battered, it lay wrecked on the runway of Luke Field.

In my life I had come to realize that when things were going very well indeed it was just the time to anticipate trouble. And, conversely, I learned from pleasant experience that at the most despairing crisis, when all looked sour beyond words, some delightful "break" was apt to lurk just around the corner.

The first gray light of day was seeping down over the eastern hills upon Pearl Harbor. From Wheeler, where we landed, we had moved to Luke Field, where a fine 3,000-foot concrete runway offered better take-off facilities. We had decided on a dawn start. It is amazing how much can happen in one dawn.

We had 900 gallons of gasoline on board. That was almost as much as we carried coming from Oakland, although the contemplated distance to Howland was 600 miles shorter than the first leg of the journey. From the reports at hand I was doubtful of weather and wanted to take along enough fuel to enable us to return after eight hours, if necessary for any reason.

However, this load was not by any means the ship's limit. Several times we had taken off comfortably with greater weight. Indeed, so easily was the plane moving down the runway that I thought the take-off was actually over. In ten seconds more we would have been off the ground, with our landing gear tucked up and on our way southwestward. There was not the slightest indication of anything abnormal.

Ten seconds later the airplane which brought us so gallantly to Honolulu lay helpless on the concrete runway, a poor battered bird with broken wings.

As for the crew, only our spirits were bruised when this sudden disaster overtook us. By good fortune, Harry Manning, Fred Noonan and I emerged without a scratch. But the plane, her landing gear wiped off and one wing damaged, was a sad sight to see. At that, the comparatively slight damage was a fine testimonial to the sturdiness of Lockheed construction—such an accident might well result in a total wash-out. It was one of those incidents in aviation which, small in themselves, may have vastly serious consequences. Witnesses said the tire blew. However, studying the tracks carefully, I believe that may not have been the primary cause of the accident. Possibly the landing gear's right shock absorber, as it lengthened, may have given way.

Watchers on the ground saw the wing drop. Suddenly the plane pulled to my right. I reduced the power on the opposite engine and succeeded in swinging from the right to the left. For a moment I thought I would be able to gain control and straighten the course. But, alas, the load was so heavy, once it started an arc there was nothing to do but let the plane ground loop as easily as possible.

With the excessive weight, the landing gear on the right was wrenched free and gasoline sprayed from the drain-well. That there was no fire was surely the result of the generous good wishes which had come to me from all over the world. No one of the three of us on board was even shaken, a testimony to the safety of a modern metal plane such as mine.

In retrospect, I am thankful that the failure occurred where it did rather than in some isolated corner of the world far from help. And I must say a good word for Fred Noonan and Harry Manning. They were both as game as could be. In fact, when the first men reached the plane and opened the cabin door, they found Fred methodically folding up his charts. He said that when I flew again he was ready to go along.

I think it was not more than two minutes after we emerged from the crack-up that I knew exactly what I wanted to do—if ways and means could be devised for doing it. My own desire, I'm sure, was set almost before the slithering slide along the concrete ended. "If we don't burn up, I want to try again." Something like that flashed through my mind. Miraculously, fire spared us. . . . The two minutes above mentioned were needed to appraise the state of the plane itself. If it were completely washed out, I knew we'd not be able to get another. If it were repairable, I thought we could carry on. Hasty examination indicated its broken bones could be mended.

"Of course now you'll give up the trip?" The speaker's inflection implied more a statement of fact than a question.

I shook my head. "I think not."

"Tough luck," another newspaperman commiserated. "Anyway, you're fortunate to be alive. By the way, I understand your husband will be greatly relieved because now you can't go on with the flight."

I knew better. Just to set the record straight, I was able later to show the inquirer a telegram sent by Mr. Putnam immediately following the accident after learning he still had a wife to wire to. This was the message: "So long as you and the boys are o.k. the rest doesnt matter. After all, it's just one of those things. Whether you want to call it a day or keep going later is equally jake with me."

That considerate spirit was "jake" with me, too! Anyway, he knew perfectly well I'd want to "keep going." Under the circumstances he'd want to himself.

I think my husband has always found a sort of grim satisfaction—a species of modern martyrdom—in being, for once, the male left behind while the female fares forth adventure-bound, thus turning topsy-turvy the accepted way of the world in such matters.

Interlude

The plane and its crew back in California, the obvious task was not to lament the past but prepare for the future.

Like broken bones which Nature knits slowly in her own special process, the injured parts of an airplane must be painstakingly restored. There is no short cut to full usefulness in either case if perfect healing is desired. In addition to "healing," a strengthening of certain members to withstand the excessive strain to which overloading subjects them was in order for my Electra. This meant some actual redesigning, another process which could not be hurried. As to the precious engines, they were already in the Pacific Airmotive shops at Burbank being thoroughly checked. After the plane and engines were together, some time would have to be allowed for testing.

With the rebuilding of the plane in hand, our next task was to appraise the effect of delay upon our flying plans. We had picked mid-March as about the best time for the flight from the standpoint of weather—so far as one could expect consistent "bests" on such a long route. Setting back the date three months would see seasons relentlessly progress. In some places progress would be with benefit to pilots, in others the reverse. Here rains began, there they abated, here winds were favorable, there monsoons and choking dust-storms were due. So we set to studying again the weather maps of the world and consulting with meteorologists who know the habits of fogs and rains and temperatures around the long equator.

The upshot of those consultations was that I decided to reverse the direction originally chosen for the flight. Earlier it had seemed that the advantage lay in passage to the west; at the later date the contrary appeared true. After all, for practical purposes and disregarding Mr. Einstein, the world measures the same distance from west to east, as east to west, on any given route.

A compelling factor in our decision was the probable imminence in the Caribbean and African areas of much less favorable weather later than early June. So it seemed sensible to get this part of the journey over as promptly as possible. Also we altered the original course which was to have been from Brazil up through Panama, Central America and Mexico. Instead of following that route I decided that the journey across the United States to Miami could be a practical shake-down flight, testing the rebuilt ship and its equipment, and thereby saving the time of running such tests in California. At Miami I knew there was fine mechanical assistance to master such "bugs" as developed in the 3,000 mile transcontinental trip.

We had worked for many months making the original plans. By reversing the route we abandoned much that had been arranged and brought a new welter of detail down upon ourselves and, I fear, considerable inconvenience to others.

Supplies of fuel and oil, spare parts and mechanics, had been spotted at many points. The revision of all this involved sundry headaches. For instance, under the original schedule there was to have been an engine overhaul at Karachi for which my Wasps would have been ripe by the time we reached there as originally planned. The very day we landed in Honolulu the technician elected for that job started by air from London to Karachi so as to be on hand in ample time. Arriving in India he was greeted by the news of our Honolulu crack-up and forthwith turned around and went home again. Naturally all that was at our expense.

Those days in April and May were full of horrid realizations like the costly Karachi excursion, forcibly driving home the sad truth that the stress and strains of an airplane accident and its aftermaths are just as severe financially as they are mechanically. On the prosaic dollar-and-cent side friends helped generously, but even so, to keep going I more-or-less mortgaged the future. Without regret, however, for what are futures for?

Revising the Pacific program was a sizeable task in itself. The Coast Guard had arranged its routine cutter cruise to Howland Island so as to be on hand there at the time of my flight, and other provisions had been made by the Navy. All that had to be worked out again, with a minimum of inconvenience to official plans.

Then there was the matter of "permissions." We had already accumulated, with the kindly co-operation of the State Department, an impressive collection of credentials. They were multitudinous and varied. In addition to routine passports and visas, in much of the territory it was necessary to secure special authority to land a plane. Here and there were forbidden regions over which one might not fly. In and over other territories no firearms or motion picture cameras were permitted. Medical credentials were necessary; pilot and navigator were swollen with a full personal cargo of vaccines and inoculations. A couple of countries required testimonial of character and a negative police record. These I contrived.

All these arrangements were made through the State Department which I surmise must grow weary of such activities foisted upon it by peripatetic pilots. Its good nature under the stress of my troublesome requests is perhaps just a normal symptom of trained diplomacy.

But before the State Department could officially act, it was necessary for me to have the approval of the Department of Commerce which has authority over civil flying. My craft had to be declared airworthy for the task in hand, and its pilot competent. It was necessary to secure this sanction all over again for the second start. It is only fair to record that the Bureau of Aeronautics probably would have preferred that I abandon the effort. Its policy was to discourage extracurricular undertakings of the kind, the common or garden term for which sometimes is "stunt flights." But having granted me permission once, the ship, personnel and flight plan being the same, it would have been difficult to withdraw it.

During these two months I was seemingly busier even than before. Nearly every day there were hours at the Lockheed plant, consulting with engineers Hibbard, Gersler and Johnson, or checking into the thousand-and-one details of the rebuilding with Harvey Christen and Firman Grey in charge of the job. With my technical adviser Paul Mantz, and the others, we worked out many refinements of technique in the installation of fuel lines, tanks, dump valves, instruments and the rest of it. Because of our changed direction and re-routing over the Caribbean, there was much to be done with our charts, mostly worked out by Fred Noonan and me.

And with all, there were pleasant interludes of domesticity involving the completion of our new home not far from the airport at Burbank, and some treasured getting-away-from-it-all visits, crammed with rest and sunshine, at Jackie Cochrane's desert ranch near Indio.

And my mail! A good way to realize how many people would like to fly around the world is to start such an undertaking and then see what the mail man brings.

Many of my most precious letters came from youngsters. To air-minded youth—especially in the lower brackets of youthfulness—a jaunt around the equator appears pretty inviting. Judging from the messages, a staggering number of boys and girls stood ready to embark with me—bless their hearts.

"I am 15 years old, 105 pounds, quiet and want to see the world. I have no money, but will work my head off. . . ." That was from Michigan.

Mostly, the volunteers ranged in age from ten to fifteen years, as many girls as boys. But there were grown-ups too. A persistent applicant listed among his qualifications that he was "a single fella" and carried "Government life insurance which is good in case killed in an airplane."

There was a sweet child in Kentucky who begged: "Please teach me to fly. . . . I will repay you if it takes the rest of my life. . . . I haven't got much because my father loads coal in a mine."

Then the custom of being "named after." It's a common phenomenon for babies to have fastened on them the names of newsworthy people, and divers infants, apparently, have been inflicted with "Amelia." But the habit doesn't stop there.

"Behind a brick plant near our home," recorded a little girl, "there is a beautiful little lake with blueish water so I named it 'Lake Amelia.' . . . I had no middle name so I adopted 'Amelia' as my middle name. I would have named my duck Amelia but since it is a he duck I can't."

A namesake I enjoyed meeting later was a Wyeth-Logan cross dark hen introduced to me at the airport in Miami. In case you don't know, that's a homing pigeon. She holds the record for the fastest flying (pigeon) in Florida—as I recall, something over fifty miles per hour. Her owner permitted me to hold and release her with what I fear must have seemed to Amelia a thoroughly unprofessional chuck into the air.

"She'll fly straight home," said Mr. Hamilton. "By the time I get back she'll be on her nest."

"A good example!" That was my husband's dour comment. "My dear, you might get pointers about this homing instinct."

Criticism, good-natured and otherwise, sometimes becomes a bit personal. I suspect it's always an open season for aviatrix. My hair, and the state it's often in, is apt to be an object of uncomplimentary comment.

The Sage of Kansas (I was born there) is concerned about that hair. Wrote William Allen White in the Emporia *Gazette,* after we'd started for Honolulu:

"Amelia Earhart is speeding across the Pacific on her round-the-world flight. She will have long boresome hours with little to do and much to think about. If we could catch her we would have just this one message, about as follows: 'Amelia dear, we knew your pappy when he was an amiable, care-free cake-eater in the University of Kansas, fifty years ago. So we have a right to take you aside and tell you something. It is this—we hope to heaven when you were packing your grip you put in a pocket comb. For you certainly need to comb your hair. Now is the time to get the tangles out and give it a good straightening. So in the long lone watches over the gray and melancholy ocean, comb your head, kid, comb your head!' "

But to return to our renewed flight plans. In retrospect I came almost to welcome our Honolulu mishap. That may have been either the mechanism of self-defensive philosophy, or just good sense. High as was the price paid, it seemed as if the knowledge gained was almost worth the cost. I mean in such things as better arrangements in navigation facilities and radio, exact reactions of the plane under heavy load conditions at various altitudes, and appreciation of its superb performance in taking off.

"Has the accident shaken your confidence?" That question was asked me many times. Its answer was clear in my mind. Nothing which happened changed my attitude towards the original project. Indeed, I felt better about the ship and its equipment than I ever did before. I was eager to fly it again.

The plane's performance had been all that could be asked. If anyone had cause to lament, it was the Electra itself. For I put burdens upon her which in normal flying she was not built to bear. She carried a heavy overload. As a matter of fact, very few times since we started our partnership have I flown her without one.

Come to think of it, most of my flying for some years has been with overloaded planes seeking distance performance. So that the problems—and the risks—of this phase of the flight were not unfamiliar to me.

Speaking of loads, the human cargo for the next flight was pared down. As Captain Manning had to return to his Atlantic command, his place as navigator was taken by Fred Noonan, whose desire to go along seemed unshaken by our experience. As to Noonan, I came to realize that there was a humanitarian aspect to the flight. Shortly before the Oakland take-off Fred was in a serious automobile accident. Soon after our return to California he survived another highway smash-up. So he and Mrs. Noonan were eager for him to take to the air for safety!

Miami

The rebuilt Electra came out of the Lockheed plant on May 19. Two days later we flew it to Oakland where our friend Elmer Dimity quietly slipped on board the cargo of "covers"* carried for philatelists.

At that time we had made no announcement of my decision to reverse the direction of the flight. It seemed sensible to slip away as quietly as we could. While I was actually heading for Miami, with hope of keeping on from there eastward, technically the journey from Burbank across the country was a shake-down flight. If difficulties developed we would bring the ship back to the Lockheed plant for further adjustments.

Accompanying me on this hop across the continent was Fred Noonan, "Bo" McKneely my mechanic, and Mr. Putnam. A leisurely afternoon's flight ended at Tucson, Arizona. The weather was sizzling hot as Arizona can be in summertime. After landing and checking in, when I started my motors again to taxi to the filling pit the left one back-fired and burst into flames. For a few seconds it was nip-and-tuck whether the fire would get away from us. There weren't adequate extinguishers ready on the ground but fortunately the Lux apparatus built in the engine killed the fire. The damage was trivial, mostly some pungently cooked rubber fittings and a deal of dirty grime. The engine required a good cleaning and the ship a face-washing.

*These had voyaged on the first flight to Honolulu and then had been returned to Oakland. They were the ship's only "payload," sold by a large New York department store in New York to collectors. The risk of final return and delivery perforce was assumed by the purchaser, whose share of the gamble was infinitesimal compared with the pilot's.

On this trip when someone asked how many times I'd flown across the continent I realized that I actually did not know. My coast-to-coast commuting has been going on for quite some years now, in planes of many sorts, from my first little Avro Avion, and an autogyro, up to the Electra. Not to mention many crossings on the air lines, and about half-a-dozen by automobile. Adding it all up, it's hard to know just when I was static enough to get much done that required doing in one place.

The next morning at Tucson a dense sandstorm blocked our way. But despite it we took off, leap-frogging at 8,000 feet over El Paso with a seemingly solid mass of sand billowing below us like a turbulent yellow sea. That night we reached New Orleans and on Sunday morning, May 23, headed on southeastward for Miami.

From New Orleans we laid a straight course across the northeasterly "corner" of the Gulf of Mexico to Tampa, a matter of about 400 miles. It was Bo's first considerable over-water flying and I am not sure he was very enthusiastic about it.

That Sunday afternoon we reached Miami, and dug in for a week of final preparation, with the generous aid of Pan American personnel.

*   *   *

(In the days that followed, A. E. had no time to write. "We'll catch up on that later," she said. "I want to do a careful account of this final job of getting ready for a long flight. It's really colorful and I think could be made interesting even for nonflyers."

The opportunity to "catch up" never came. Instead of filling in myself, I've chosen to present something of the story of that week before departure in words written at the time by C. B. Allen of the New York *Herald Tribune,* a good friend who was with us at Miami.

G.P.P.)

*   *   *

"Those who had an opportunity to observe Miss Earhart at Miami in final preparations for her round-the-world flight could not help being impressed by the calm and unhurried manner in which she made sure that everything about her ship was as ready as expert technicians could make it before she would consider starting the trip.

There was no hurrying or harassing of mechanics to finish their work so that she might take off at a given time, no slightest indication of impatience when a difficult job took longer to finish than might have been expected.

"It was interesting to watch the effect of such an attitude on the Pan American Airways mechanics and others who were assigned to give Miss Earhart whatever assistance they could. Being men and being engaged in a highly essential phase of the serious business of air transportation, they all naturally had preconceived notions about a woman pilot bent on a 'stunt' flight—not very favorable notions, either. It was, undoubtedly, something of a shock to discover that the 'gal' with whom they had to deal not only was an exceptionally pleasant and reasonable human being who 'knew her stuff,' but that she knew exactly what she wanted done, and had sense enough to let them alone while they did it. There was an almost audible clatter of chips falling off skeptical masculine shoulders.

"Any lingering doubts were dispelled when it developed that this particular woman aviator not only was thoroughly familiar with every part of her airplane, but was not above helping push it in and out of the hangar or lending a hand on any job where it was needed or her advice or presence was required. A little grease or oil on her olive drab slacks or plaid, short-sleeved shirt, or even in her tousled hair habitually was dismissed by Miss Earhart with a chuckle when anyone called her attention to the matter.

"It did not escape the sharp-eyed mechanics that autograph seekers and photographers who hovered about the municipal airport inevitably caught up with the air-woman rather than her catching up with them, and that, while she was unfailingly good-natured and obliging, she ducked these incidents as much as possible. Habitually gracious both to these representatives of her 'public' and to the technicians working on her plane, Miss Earhart conducted herself simply and naturally, showing no irritation, even on occasions when she must have felt it, and refusing at all times to resort to the technique called 'turning on the charm.'

"Ordinarily when there was a prospect that she would be needed to take her ship up to test its equipment, she ate lunch at the 'greasy spoon' restaurant across the highway from the airport and reported her pleased discovery that the food was as good as that at downtown hotels. She was particularly delighted to find out that the 'greasy spoon' served rich, creamy buttermilk, flecked with bits of butter—her favorite beverage.

"At intervals during her stay she protested plaintively that she wanted to take time out for a swim and a sun bath, 'but I just don't get a chance.' She got several roastings from the blistering tropical sun while sitting in the pilot's cabin of her all-metal plane on the airport testing its instruments and engines, but insisted that this was 'not the same thing at all as a good sun bath; I want to soak up a little sunshine, not be fried by it.'

"Probably the best time Miss Earhart had in Miami was when she visited the Pan American Airways' international air terminal and maintenance base at Dinner Key and was taken for a tour of the big hangar-workshops where the company's Sikorsky Clipper ships are hauled out of the water for inspection after each flight, and periodically overhauled. Her escort on this occasion was W. G. Richards, the air line's chief mechanic, who, like all the other workmen who came into contact with Miss Earhart, appeared to have been completely sold on her ability and personality.

"Mr. Richards fairly glowed under Miss Earhart's expert appraisal of the 'amazing efficiency' apparent in every department of the maintenance base, and the willingness with which all Pan American personnel assigned to work on her ship kept at the job attested how relieved they were to discover that she was something other than 'a temperamental woman who thinks she can fly.'

"Noonan, of course, renewed a lot of old acquaintances during the visit to Dinner Key, being one of the oldest veterans of the Pan American system, and it was interesting to see his friends' attitude changing in light of their firsthand observations of Miss Earhart. Previously they had been inclined to feel a little bit sorry for 'poor old Fred, flying around the world like this with a woman pilot'; now they were willing to concede that 'poor old Fred' needed no sympathy, that he evidently had signed up with 'the pick of the lot' of women aviators, just as they believe that she chose one of the best aerial navigators in the world."[1]

---

[1] In a letter sent to his wife at Oakland when the flight had run about half its scheduled course, Fred Noonan wrote: "Amelia is a grand person for such a trip. She is the only woman flyer I would care to make such an expedition with. Because in addition to being a fine companion and pilot, she can take hardship as well as a man—and work like one."

(Those who knew A. E. best, and especially those who saw her working with the men who were preparing her ship, realized her delight in the job at hand. She was seldom happier, I think, than when perched on a service-stand watching some adjustment of her beloved engines, or sprawled on the concrete tarmac observing experts wrestle with a troublesome strut or dump valve. And probably as grimy as a grease monkey. . . . It's illuminating to record what she'd planned for her first "party" following her return, a characteristic house-warming of her new home in Southern California. The guests were to be exclusively the men (and their wives) who had worked on her plane, the gang who had "put out" the best they had, in hours and out of hours, at the Lockheed plant, at Union Air Terminal, and at Oakland. She had a full list of them. They were the ones whose help she wanted them to know she appreciated.

G.P.P.)

Prior to that dawn of June first, when A. E. took her silver plane up into the sunrise at Miami, she confided a secret. Before getting on with its pilot's story of Last Flight itself, I close this chapter with this brief piece of Carl Allen's, written by him later:

"Amelia Earhart's equatorial flight around the world was to have been her last great aerial adventure—a final fling at spectacular flying before she settled down to the more or less prosaic existence of participation in routine phases of aviation. She confided this to one or two friends just before she started.

" 'I have a feeling that there is just about one more good flight left in my system,' she said, 'and I hope this trip is it. Anyway, when I have finished this job, I mean to give up long-distance "stunt" flying.'

"Miss Earhart hastened to add that this was by no means an announcement of an intended retirement from flying. On the contrary, she said that she meant to continue flying in connection with her lecturing and other work, and that one of the first things she wanted to do after completing a world flight was to carry out an extensive flight research program at Purdue University.

" 'But the fact that you are through with long-distance air exploits when this flight is over is a darned good news story,' Miss Earhart was reminded. 'Why can't that be written as soon as you are safely on your way?'

"She shook her head. She said that she was constitutionally opposed to advance announcements any more than was absolutely necessary; that 'so many things can happen' to change one's program 'or even a woman's mind.' With what soon had the appearance of uncanny foresight.

" 'If you use that story at all, wait until the round-the-world flight is over, or nearly over; I think it would be absurd to make such an announcement now, especially if I should be forced to give up my present program or to postpone it, for any reason, when I had only just started.'

"Miss Earhart said that her decision to retire from the stunt-flying arena was prompted by a number of reasons. Among them was the repeated urging of her husband that she give up hazardous flight attempts, her own feeling that she had done her fair share in this field and the growing conviction 'that I'm getting old and want to make way for the younger generation before I'm feeble, too.' "

The Start

On June 1, at 5:56 in the morning, NR 16020 left Municipal Airport at Miami with Fred Noonan aboard as navigator and I as pilot, bound for California by about the longest route we could contrive.

At the very last there was a delay while Bo McKneely, my mechanic, resoldered a broken thermocouple lead which supplied the cylinder head temperatures of the left engine. While this went on, all warmed up and plenty of places to go, we sat for a last breathing spell on the concrete apron beside the hangar watching the rising sun brush back the silver gray of dawn.

The tinkering job completed, back in place went the cowling.

"Okeh," said Bo.

Fred climbed in the cockpit and my husband, standing alongside on the wing center-section, leaned in and bade me good-by. I closed and fastened the hatch. The gathering crowd safely distant from the propellar blades, ground attendants signaled "All clear." In a last look through the window I spied nearby the Viking blond head of Mr. Putnam's son, David, and waved to him. Then I started the motors.

The engines had already been well warmed so now after appraising for a moment their full-throated smooth song, I signaled to have the wheel chocks removed and we taxied to the end of the runway in the far southeast corner of the field. Thirty seconds later, with comforting ease, we were in the air and on our way.

After the take-off for thirteen minutes we climbed slowly, swinging on our course toward Puerto Rico. Beautiful in the early morning light was the curving line made where the blue depths of the Gulf Stream met the aquamarine of the shoal waters off the coast.

Now and then as we flew along I thought we glimpsed the outlines of shadowy fish, dark against the pale sand below. Legend has it that sailfish are found thereabouts. I say "legend" because our one day's fishing from Miami, when we played hookey from airport chores, was totally unsuccessful. Neither on the fringes of the Gulf Stream nor elsewhere did we capture a single fish of any kind. So to me their existence remains merely hearsay, though I am more than willing to give my enthusiastic Florida friends the benefit of every doubt—even to the point of agreeing that, as someone cruelly remarked, "as a fisherman Miss Earhart is a good pilot."

Shortly after six o'clock two ships were visible. It was then, with them beneath us, when everything in the cockpit was properly set and working smoothly, I tuned in on Miami's radio station WQAM, which was broadcasting every hour a summary of weather conditions which lay before us, as prepared by Pan American's efficient meterologists. My own schedule called for a broadcast every thirty minutes at a quarter past and a quarter to the hour.

I was delayed a little with my first broadcast because just then the radio station was sending out a description of my own take-off, which to me was quite too entertaining to miss. The masterpiece was evidently transcribed from a description made by an announcer at the field. The actual take-off hour being too early for most civilized stay-a-bed Miamians, the record was now being played on the air again for their delectation while they ate their breakfasts and we winged southward.

So, a hundred miles from the field, the announcer held me in cruel suspense as to whether or not I actually was going to get off safely! It was diverting to hear that third-person story. In the manner radio-folk sometimes have, the account of the very normal departure had become breathlessly exciting.

As the sun rose higher, the sea became hazy. A few fuzzy clouds sailed lazily beneath the silver wings of the ship. Fred Noonan was not enjoying the scenery as such, but spotting conformations of the islands beneath us, and looking for lighthouses with which to check our course and rate of speed. From P.A.A. experience, all this was ground—and water—well-known to him.

At six-thirty we sighted the great reef of the Bahama banks. At about seven o'clock, Andros Island stretched out as a vivid green rug before our eyes. The fringe of that rug was formed by the var-icolored tendrils of the sea reaching fingerlike into the islands, some resembling vivid green snakes wriggling in a maritime Garden of Eden.

The beauties of these tropic seas viewed from the air were in sharp contrast to the leaden dullness of the North Atlantic and far reaches of the Pacific Ocean, as I have seen them from aloft.

My penciled log, scribbled in the cockpit as we flew, records that off Andros we sighted a partly submerged wreck, mute testimony of a tragedy of long ago. Also such lines as these: "We look down upon little rocks and reefs which just poke their heads above the water. . . . So few lighthouses in this mess—one pities the poor mariner. . . . On some solider ground we saw trees in black silhouette against the burnished sunpath. . . . A friendly course. Hardly out of sight of one island but another pancakes on the horizon. . . . The shadows of clouds (white clouds in the blue sky) are like giant flowers, dark on the green sea. . . . Curtains of rain clouds aloft . . . the sun shines weakly through the overcast which keeps down temperature; at 4800 feet it is only 80 degrees outside. . . . Sperry has been flying much of the time. . . . Tuned in at about 1300 on a Spanish station and heard my name. . . . Sea and sky are indistinguishable; there is nothing to see. . . . F. N. smells land."

Cumulus clouds piled high, their shadows floating across the pale waters. Flying at a thousand feet, we sneaked beneath some of these cloud layers, soon emerging again into brilliance. It was a pretty game of hide-and-seek with the sun.

By mid-morning, Noonan had estimated that we would reach San Juan by ten minutes past one o'clock. I remembered a few days earlier, while we were still far from land flying across the Gulf of Mexico he had predicted we would sight Tampa at 12:10. Actually we made our landfall one minute earlier. So I had come to have implicit faith in my shipmate's powers of divination.

What with such expert navigational help and the assistance of the Sperry gyropilot, I began to feel that my long-range flying was becoming pretty sissy. The ease and casualness were further accentuated by the marvelous help given by radio. Were I alone on such a trip as this, I would be hopping along shorelines, my attention divided between flying the ship and attempting to keep track of exactly where I was.

At about noon Navigator Noonan told me we were too far south and I changed my course as directed. At the moment there was nothing to see but indistinguishable sea and sky. And then suddenly through a haze we sighted Puerto Rico. That was just after noon. Checking the time, I was reminded that I'd eaten nothing at all since the before-dawn breakfast at a lunch-counter in Miami, a thousand miles behind us. Later, Fred told me he had indulged in one sandwich and some coffee.

Following along the shoreline we came soon to the airport, close beside the colorful city of San Juan. It was odd to see a four-masted schooner anchored practically just off the runway. Later I found she had brought cod from Nova Scotia to return "down east" with Turks Island salt.

Once on the ground the matter of my neglected meal very promptly was attended to, our luncheon hostess being Mrs. Thomas Rodenbaugh, wife of the Pan American manager.

Acting Governor Menendez Ramos generously offered hospitality, but we had made arrangements to impose ourselves upon a fellow pilot who was on hand to greet us. She—as my husband sometimes says, "Women pilots pop up from under stones 'most anywhere"—was Miss Clara Livingston, one of the few private flyers on the island. Once the formalities of our arrival and the grooming of the Electra were cared for, we drove out to Clara's plantation, twenty miles from town.

A great advantage in visiting a pilot is knowing that one's host comprehends a pilot's needs. Which, when much flying lies ahead, are mostly negative. By which I mean *not* having things done for one, and instead being allowed to do nothing. Which sounds involved, but perhaps isn't. We wanted quiet and sleep. When politely possible, it was helpful to avoid functions and people—even the pleasantest people, for meeting and talking to them adds immeasurably to the fatigue factor, nervous and physical.

Clara proved the perfect hostess. Her hospitality under the circumstances was exactly right. She stoically resisted all temptation involving social trimmings. She had only one complaint. Fred, it appears, insulted her view. Sitting on the front balcony, despite the lovely tropic vista before him, he went sound asleep.

In our ears that evening was the surge of the sea at the very front door, background for the soothing song of frogs and night insects. No sounds of traffic, no radio, in Clara's sixteen hundred acre queendom, and straight northward no neighbor all the way to Greenland.

One conversation I did have that night, before our eight o'clock going-to-bed. That was by telephone with my husband, who talked from the office of Ellis Hollums in the *Herald* office in Miami. It appeared that the little account of our day's progress which I had sent to the cable office to be forwarded to newspapers had not gone. I never did discover whether the local operator just didn't think it was worth bothering with. At that, he was probably correct. It's hard to turn correspondent after one has been a pilot all day. . . . But especially, I suspect, Mr. Putnam just wanted to say "Good night." That was pleasant.

At San Juan by the way, I was asked, as often, just why I was attempting the flight, and especially why on this second start I had delayed announcing my intention of proceeding eastward. The answers, such as they are, are perhaps worth repeating here.

So much was written before and after the March 17 take-off at Oakland, and following the Honolulu accident, that I thought it would be a pleasant change just to slip away without comment. The extent of the publicity accompanying the first start was unsolicited and doubtless more than the flight deserved even if it had been successful.

The fact is that the career of one who indulges in any kind of flying off the beaten path is often complicated. For instance, if one gives out plans beforehand, one is likely to be charged with publicity seeking by those who do not know how difficult it is to escape the competent gentlemen of the press. On the other hand, if one slips away, as I have generally tried to do, the slipper-away invites catcalls from those who earn their living writing and taking photographs.

So I am hoping the pros and cons of the whole undertaking can wait until it is finally over. If I am successful, the merits and demerits can be threshed out then. If not, someone else will do what I have attempted and I'll pass the problem on to him—or her.

To Paramaribo

From San Juan I had hoped perhaps to be able to fly through in one day to Paramaribo in Dutch Guiana. But that did not work out and instead we spent the night at Caripito in Venezuela.

While the air courses of the Caribbean and along the coasts of South America are well traveled by the ships of Pan American Airways, which have established a notably successful record with their southern service, it must be remembered that P.A.A. flies seaplanes so that all the way they have a watery landing strip beneath them where they may alight. For a land plane, however, especially a rather large one requiring considerable space on alighting, this territory is more difficult. On the three-thousand-mile stretch from San Juan to Natal there are only four reasonably satisfactory airports and between them the slimmest sort of chance for a ship like mine to land safely. The intermediate territory mostly offers the alternative of Atlantic Ocean or jungled tree-tops.

At Clara Livingston's plantation in Puerto Rico I rolled out of bed at a quarter of four in the morning, hoping to make a dawn take-off from San Juan, but actually the Electra did not lift her wheels from the runway until nearly seven o'clock, with the sun well above the horizon. Incidentally, construction work at the field shortened the available take-off distance, making a heavy fuel load a bit difficult, and adding a further factor in the final decision not to try to push through the thousand miles to Paramaribo.

"*Push through.*" I find myself writing those words almost resentfully. We're always pushing through, hurrying on our long way, trying to get to some other place instead of enjoying the place we'd already got to. A situation, alas, about which there was no use complaining.

I'd made my schedule and had to abide by it. After all, this was not a voyage of sight-seeing. Only there were so many sights I wanted to see. These lovely white Caribbean cities, for instance, nestling among green hills.

As to San Juan, I had a curious feeling I had been there before—which I hadn't! But at least I left determined to visit it again. All the way, the amibition strengthened to retrace my steps (what is the aviation synonym for that—"re-fly my courses"?), next time really seeing the lands I've only skimmed now—all of them entirely new to me—and visiting their peoples in a decently leisurely and civilized manner. Sometime I hope to stay somewhere as long as I like.

In Puerto Rico and our South American stops I noticed first what was further borne in on me as we progressed eastward. We had chosen a route which lay in lands of exclusively brown-eyed people. All the native eyes, seemingly, were dark. I began deliberately looking for blue eyes. It was a little like the childhood game of spotting white horses as one drove the highways, or the more sophisticated beard-hunting pastime, "Beaver."

From the time we crossed the green mountains of Puerto Rico until we sighted the Island of Margarita to starboard we saw nothing but the tops of clouds and the blue sea below. A line in my log-book: "The little clouds spread far. They looked like white scrambled eggs." I flew at 8,000 feet most of the way, bucking head winds of probably thirty miles an hour.

The coast of Venezuela in the hazy distance was my first glimpse of South America. As we drew near I saw densely wooded mountains and between them wide valleys of open plains and jungle. I had never seen a jungle before. Like the purple cow which one would rather see than be, close-knit tropic jungles are in a pilot's eyes about the least desirable of all possible landing places. Planes have, on occasion, pan-caked more-or-less in one piece into (or upon) the tree-tops, and the pilot been able to "walk away," as the saying goes. But such walking (if any) in a genuine jungle! Likely, the getting away would be worse than the getting down.

A muddy river wound through the mountain pass we followed, a reddish-brown snake crawling among tight-packed greenery. A few miles inland lay the red-roofed town of Caripito, with squat oil tanks on the outskirts. There was a splendid airfield, with paved runways and a well-equipped hangar. It is managed jointly by Pan American

Airways and the Standard Oil Company. We were met by Don Andres Rolando, President of the state of Monagas, and Don Ramiro Rendiles, Secretary-General, who were accompanied by their wives. They welcomed us cordially to their beautiful country.

While the Electra was appropriately refreshed with gasoline, its crew were guests at a luncheon prepared and served in the hangar. An elaborate and delicious meal it was, running the gastronomic gamut from grape juice to beefsteak and fruitcake. Our host was Henry E. Linam, general manager of the Standard Oil Company of Venezuela, at whose home we stayed. It seems that hospitality always awaits flying visitors.

At my place at the table were orchids such as denizens of drab cities to the north wear only on extravagant occasions. In this lush country the lovely blooms grow wild, as commonplace as the poppies of California. Mine seemed beautiful even against the dingy setting of a crumpled flying shirt.

Rain clouds hung thick about Caripito as we left on the morning of June third. We flew over jungles to the coast, and then played hide-and-seek with showers until I decided I had better forgo the scenery, such as it was, and climb up through the clouds into fair weather. An altitude of 8,000 feet topped all but the highest woolly pinnacles.

In such a maneuver lies a recurrent delight of flying. Often one can find the weather wanted, at one level or another. As on this and many other days, the pilot sees the rain slant against the land below. Horizontally, distant views are blotted out; vertically, clouds droop to shroud the shoulders of mountains, or weep upon the jungled plain. But how many of the earthbound realize the relative nearness of sunlight above the cloud-covering? How many know that perhaps only three thousand feet above the gray dank world my plane, if I will it, may emerge into sunlight over a billowy sea of clouds stretching away into blue infinity.

Sometimes the climb is greater, sometimes the airplane cannot top the towering formation of a storm. But no matter whether separated by ice or snow or rain or cold gray mist, the pilot knows the wall-card motto is meteorologically true, "Behind the clouds the sun's still shining."

Now and again that sun illumines mystic caves and rearing fortresses or shows giant cloud creatures mocking with lumpy paws the tiny man-made bird among them. But the airman's pleasantest sight is probably glimpses of the earth through openings in a cloudy floor beneath his wings.

Such sights in plenty we had in the days that followed, of sea and jungle and shoreline, framed by the clouds that played tag with us during most of our hours aloft.

When we sighted Georgetown, British Guiana, we were well out at sea cutting corners, but even so we could distinguish the neat irrigated fields around the settlement and along the coast. Between the two Guianas, British and Dutch, was a wide muddy delta into which flowed the river Nickerie. Indeed, the entire coastal region abounds with sprawling jungle waterways, many of them connected to each other by cross-streams.

Later, we cut more corners, inland. While Fred Noonan had flown this region many times, our route differed from those he had followed before. In a letter home he wrote: "The flight from Caripito to Paramaribo was tremendously interesting. Instead of following the coastline as Pan American seaplanes do and I have always done before, we cut straight across dense virgin jungle. It was so thick that for hundreds of miles all we could see was solid tree-tops broken by an occasional large river."

Strong head winds again cut the speed to an average of 148 miles, which included dodging squalls and flying low. I cannot make fast time at a low altitude, other conditions being the same, for it is too hard on the engines to open the throttles wide when near the ground, except momentarily on a take-off. Modern engines attain an efficiency so high that I certainly would not knowingly mistreat my faithful ones. Today's geography required the best equipment for safety.

As we progressed, the clouds disappeared and I began to descend for sightseeing again. From an uninhabitable swampy shore endless armies of jungle trees marched inland. Then clearings, where many little houses appeared among the paddy fields.

Soon we saw the river Surinam, a silver streak meandering to the coast, a wide tidal stream full of floating green islands of small trees and water plants, and bordered with vast stretches of mud. Twelve miles from its mouth is Paramaribo, capital of Dutch Guiana, and twenty-five miles further inland the airport.

Our instructions were to follow a narrow-gauge railroad track. Flying very low, we rounded every curve even as Casey Jones did.

Nothing was visible but engulfing jungle stretching endlessly with little rice fields and huts beside the track. I tried to see the wind direction from smoke or from clothes on lines, as I expected to find only a meager clearing, and felt I might have to sit down suddenly.

Then in a matter of minutes, the field. Such a pleasant surprise! No make-shift airport this, but one of the best natural landing areas I have ever seen, where everything possible was prepared for our arrival with what one is apt to set down appreciatively as characteristic Dutch thoroughness.

An orange wind sock flew from a pole. Strips of white cloth marked the best section for landing. As soon as we came into view, a bonfire was touched off to show the wind direction and a man waved a white flag to guide us in. "Zandery" is the field's name, which means "sandy." As far as I could see it is the only space of the kind for miles.

We were welcomed by Commissary Wempe and Captain Sluyter, in command of troops, James Lawton, American Consul at Paramaribo, and others who had come out from town. Soldiers stood by to pump in gasoline from drums and guard the plane. Coffee, orange juice and sandwiches were ready for hot and famished flyers. Never did I have better service anywhere, or welcome more sincere.

After the tanks had been refilled and the propellers greased, the plane was staked down in the open, for there was no hangar. Then we embarked on the railroad which we had followed in from the coast for the hour's run to Paramaribo. Dogs, chickens and goats were herded from the track at our approach. Women carrying baskets of fruit on their heads came to the car when we stopped. For part of the way, the road ran beside a canal. Burma cattle, burros, bicycles, a fleet of boats and, now and then, automobiles, were varied means of locomotion noted.

The next day we had planned a jump to Fortaleza, Brazil, though that depended on the weather and field conditions. It had rained heavily at Paramaribo the previous day but the officials solemnly promised to arrange a good take-off wind and dry ground in the early morning as part of their hospitality.

The name of the river, Surinam, was once applied to this whole country. In its heyday, Surinam was a black spot of slavery and colorful viciousness, probably as wicked a town as flourished along all the wild coast of South America.

The Paramaribo of today is a substantial community with the inherent virtues of Holland written in its broad tree-planted streets and its general spic-and-spanness. But, at that, it is picturesquely tropical. The adjacent jungle, which creeps to the very edge of town, is inhabited by Bush Negroes, descendants of escaped African slaves of long ago. Now they are a friendly people and it was fun to glimpse them in the market, bartering soft-shell turtle eggs, string beans eighteen inches long, horned cucumbers, breadfruit and sapodillas.

We stayed at the Palace Hotel, a stamping ground of Noonan's in his P.A.A. days. Here he encountered an old friend, Carl Doake, who was his radio operator in Haiti in 1930.

This South American leg of our journey provided a sort of old-home week for Fred, who knew many people and was familiar with the coast line generally although he did not know the land-plane fields we used. Incidentally, little by little I came to know my shipmate's full story.

In addition to being an air navigator, he is a Master Mariner unlimited. And, for some quaint reason, he also holds a first-class pilot's license on the Mississippi River. In his diversified twenty-odd years of nautical knocking about, he rounded Cape Horn seven times, thrice on a wind-jammer and four times on steamships. At the age of fifteen for no particularly good reason except that he wanted to, Fred left home to go to sea. During the World War he served on a munitions carrier between New York and England, and later in the British Navy was on three ships which were torpedoed.

Once we were discussing the delays apparently inevitable in aviation, especially with our kind of flying.

"It's all a matter of comparison," Fred assured me. "We're impatient about a day's delay. That's because that lost day's flying might see us across a continent or an ocean. But a swell way to learn patience is to try a tour of sailing-ship voyaging. Back in 1910 I was on the bark *Crompton* which was then the largest square-rigged ship under the English flag. We were weather-bound 152 days on the voyage from the state of Washington, on the Pacific coast, to Ireland. After nearly half a year on one vessel on one trip you become pretty philosophical about the calendar!"

At that, I decided to stick to airplanes.

Fortaleza and Natal

The weather at Paramaribo was perfect except for a morning mist from the Surinam River, when we took off to skim the tree-tops and then pull up.

Speaking of trees, we had plenty of them on this jump to Fortaleza in Brazil—trees and water. During the day we flew over 960 miles of jungle, added to hops of 370 miles by compass course over open sea, a total of 1,330 miles, or a trifle more than half the transcontinental distance between New York and Los Angeles.

There was only one possible stop between Paramaribo and Fortaleza, a jungle-surrounded and none-too-large field at Para, which, as all went well, we passed by. The infrequency of ports of call made land-plane flying somewhat uncertain as I've pointed out. Then, again, we left too early to receive weather reports so what lay in store for us was largely a matter of conjecture. Under such conditions in a strange country one must be prepared to turn back if and when it looks like bad visibility at the destination—assuming the way back can be found and a landing made wherever "back" may be.

Yesterday I had my introduction to a continent new to me. Today I crossed the equator for the first time. Fred had plotted an appropriate ceremony, himself officiating as an aerial King Neptune. But at the time the Electra's shadow passed over the mythical Line we were both so occupied he quite forgot to duck me with the thermos bottle of cold water which he later confessed had been provided for the occasion.

I remember once crossing the United States by night, when I had been flying very high, glimpsing through suddenly opening clouds the broad Mississippi gleaming in the moonlight. Today we crossed the Mississippi's southern brother, the huge Amazon. We did not actually span the river itself, short-cutting the 180 mile stretch between the capes at its ultimate mouth. To our right stretched the lower delta, seen from aloft a crazy-quilt of variously colored currents each flowing its chosen course, each retaining its own particular hue of yellow or brown muddiness, and all bearing seaward, like matches, countless thousands of giant trees wrenched up at the roots. How far beyond our view those tentacles of muddy water soiled the sea I do not know.

After about ten hours' flying I was glad to see Fortaleza sitting just where it should be, according to the maps, between the mountains and the sea, on a brown, sandy plain, in the arc of a crescent-shaped indentation just west of Cape Mucuripe. The adjacent coast line differed vastly from that encountered northward. Instead of dank jungles surging down to the surf there were wide stretches of semi-desert, and off-shore tidal flats of mud and sandy reefs. Here the climate was almost arid. Drought, not excessive rainfall, was customary.

Fortaleza is a town of 100,000 people, a potent metropolis whose name few of us in North America have even heard. In my own ignorance I had thought of Natal as a more important place. That, of course, because Natal figures so largely in aviation matters.

Fortaleza's airport was so fine we decided to make final preparations for the South Atlantic hop there rather than at Natal, the actual jumping-off place for that much-flown stretch. When Captain Macedo generously put at our disposal Pan American Airways' facilities we determined to lay over a day and get everything shipshape with the plane, mechanically and from a housekeeping standpoint. Likewise ourselves. Sartorially, at least, we required a full measure of attention. Looking as we did after only a week on the way, I hesitated to visualize what disgraceful tramps we'd be before journey's end.

With the plane the only specific job to be done, so far as appeared, was curing one small leak where a gauge let flow a few drops of gasoline, though from a harmless source. But while everything was working well, a complete inspection was in order, and an oil change, greasing, check of landing gear and the like. Further, the plane itself was given a thorough-going scrubbing. Moisture of the preceding week had tarnished its metal surfaces, which every so often should be cleaned and burnished to a degree.

Laundrying for ourselves seemed as important as for the plane. I was on my last shirt and had abandoned hope that the appearance of my slacks, or my shoes, ever again would be respectable. (Phil Cooper,* I am sure, would have disowned me.) My one suitcase supposedly carried everything I could need on a world flight but of necessity it didn't contain many duplications. My wardrobe included five shirts, two pairs of slacks, a change of shoes, a light working coverall and a trick weightless raincoat, plus the minimum of toilet articles. Which, for me, was pretty elaborate. In my salad days I flew the Atlantic with no luggage at all and no personal equipment but a toothbrush. A reward was the fun of shopping in London literally "from the bottom up."

And a sun helmet. Neither Fred nor I have a coat (which complicates formal entertaining). But soundly lectured by tropical experts, wise in the ways of sun-stroke, we each started with one sun hat, to which others, as gifts, were added seemingly at each port of call. By habit we are both bare-headed people and I find each of us up to this point apparently had worn one hat once, and that solely because whenever we fared forth friends clapped protective headgear on our unworldly pates.

In Fortaleza we stayed at the Excelsior Hotel.** The windows of our rooms opened on red-tiled roofs and busy streets which ended in the sea. I could hardly believe we were in the tropics it was so comfortably cool, with a good breeze. But after all I know the tropics only from books, and I have always loved sunshine and warmth.

---

*Phil is a New York cleaner who has kept A. E.'s outfits comparatively presentable for years. He endeared himself at the conclusion of the Atlantic solo flight by sending her this message: "Knew you'd make it. I never lost a customer."

**In one of the few letters she had time to write, A. E. reported from Fortaleza: "The hotel people naïvely put F. N. and me in the same room. They were a bit surprised when we both countermanded the arrangements! . . . For a female to be traveling as I do evidently is a matter of puzzlement to her sheltered sisters hereabout, not to mention the males. I'm stared at in the streets. I feel they think, 'Oh, well, she's American and they're all crazy.' " G.P.P.

At the airport next day Fred and I cleaned house while the men worked on the plane. We repacked all spares, sent home the maps used so far and washed the oily engine and propeller covers. These, of light strong Grenfell cloth, I had designed and made at Burbank. They were close-fitting union suits to protect engines and propellers from sand and dust, and somewhat from rain, when absence of hangar facilities made it necessary to stake out our chariot for the night. Also we sorted what we had accumulated in the last few days, including everything from a gift pineapple to calling cards, and one unusual object—a large yellow and mauve moth who had established himself on the black cushions of a pilot's seat. I wondered if it had recognized the Wasp-motored Lockheed Electra monoplane as a very big brother.

Among our purchases were coveralls for Navigator Noonan, a transaction whose bewildering speed would put to shame any North American tailor shop I've encountered. He was measured for them at eleven o'clock in a shop where ten or more women sat at sewing machines, ready to pounce on the cloth as soon as it was cut. By afternoon he was properly garbed to do any kind of manual labor. I had brought along my own suit.

Fortaleza is one of two cities in Brazil which is laid out with straight streets. I found that out when I left the airplane long enough to do some exploring, in addition to shopping. The latter included a successful search for sponge rubber to replace some on the cockpit hatch which was wearing out. A pleasant feature of the purchase was that I was not permitted to pay for it.

I found on Fortaleza's waterfront interesting sights. The fishermen were returning with the day's catch in catamarans called "jangada." Most of these are very small, consisting of logs bound together, with a large three-cornered sail overhead. The mariners venture as far as twenty miles off-shore and are famous for their skill in handling their frail craft. Great, round, hand-made baskets lashed to the masts were the usual containers for the fish. Sale of the wares began as soon as the boats were beached and hauled on rollers back under the palm trees which line the shore, an open-air market colorful and pungent.

The dexterity of the fishermen is not more than that of the women I saw balancing varied loads on their heads while they paced along, their hands and arms occupied with large or small bundles, or baskets with fruit or loaves of bread. The only inconvenience seems to be their inability to turn their heads quickly if anything worth looking at passes. The custom appears to aid the carriage, for they are straight and sturdy as can be.

I went tourist and took pictures of burros loaded with produce and human beings. They wear an ingenious combination of pannier and saddle and carry staggering loads. For Fortaleza, businesslike and bustling as it is, abounds in contrast. Buses, street cars and automobiles rub fenders with primitive carts and the laboring donkeys. Decrepit buildings roofed with ancient weathered tile stand beside examples of modern construction and architecture. And over the beach where the primitive catamarans set sail, roar airplanes bound for Miami, Buenos Aires and beyond.

Cows seem to have a special place about the fringes of my flying. A group of them were munching breakfast in the heavy grass at the edge of Fortaleza's airport when we appeared at dawn. They just didn't like the commotion created by the Electra's engines warming up. They showed their hurt feelings not by silly protest, but by gravely stalking away, turning a completely cold shoulder (plus hind-quarters) on the interloper. Proud cows, those. Likely they were kin to some haughty hero of the bull-ring.

During the night a deluge of rain had fallen and I feared we might find the field a quagmire. But fortunately it was well drained and the sod hard and firm. So there was no difficulty in getting off the light load needed for the short 270 mile hop to Natal.

We got into the air at 4:50 A.M. and arrived at Natal at 6:55, so our day's work was done almost before conventional breakfast time. However, we had wanted to reach Natal early, on the chance we might start thence across the South Atlantic that evening.

The weather was unsettled all the way, a morning of vagrant clouds and rain-squalls which chased each other across the sky. It was interesting country we flew over. Ruffled dunes on the shore shone with bright sand. We passed near a stately church on a high hill, supposed to be one of the oldest in Brazil. We could see it plainly and even spot parishioners, tiny dark dots trailing along the white ribbon of a road.

We saw the airport at Natal almost before the town because it is so large, consisting of long marked runways, large hangars and living quarters. With French, German, Brazilian and American planes coming and going constantly it is, I suppose, the most cosmopolitan and multilingual airfield of our hemisphere.

In the last few minutes of flying we raced a black rain squall to the field. As we turned on the runway and taxied toward the hangar the rain caught us, a muddy tropic deluge which blotted out vision fifty feet away. We were waterproof in our cockpit, but those who kindly rushed out to push the plane into shelter were soaked for their pains.

The French have been crossing the South Atlantic on regular schedule for several years. The service is now run twice a week, carrying mail but no passengers. I talked with the crew of the next plane out, and found they preferred to fly early in the morning, since they expect the most difficult weather during the first 800 miles.

So I decided to rely on their experience and defer my departure until the following morning, by which is meant some time after midnight. The plane was refueled by daylight so as to be ready. If the weather had turned out too bad to take off in the dark with such a heavy load, I planned to wait until the next afternoon and then fly all night, reaching Africa in the morning.

Everyone at Natal co-operated generously. The French have two ships stationed in the South Atlantic, which give weather conditions, and their information they shared with me. Incidentally, I believe that a similar arrangement will be—at least should be—worked out in connection with the North Atlantic flying services. In due time we may well see a couple of vessels anchored at appropriate positions to serve as gatherers of weather data, as radio guideposts and emergency aids. Perhaps such a system may involve the use of modified "floating landing fields" which were considerably discussed some years ago.

The soil in this part of Brazil is red, reminiscent of Georgia or Virginia. As many of the houses are built of 'dobe a vivid touch of color is added to the landscape. Green trees face a gray-green sea.

At luncheon I could hardly realize that I was in South America, for the food was so like that at home—corn on the cob and apple pie à la mode. Speaking of food, everyone took pity on us. When we left Fortaleza we had a present of a package of turkey sandwiches and cake. If this continues there will be no keeping down our weight, lean as Fred and I naturally are. By the way, the measuring stick of avoirdupois aloft is gasoline. Six added pounds offset one precious gallon of fuel.

As I write this, looking out the window I can see two children playing in the sand. I would like to play too, or at least sunbake beside them. Beyond, the surf beats against a stranded wreck. I noticed a number of these along the coast, and the long white ribbons of surf breaking on the shoals and sandbars that lurk dangerously about twenty-five miles off the shore.

I want to get a pair of sandals such as I see so many people wearing. It is easy to understand where this season's toeless and heelless shoes originated—somewhere around the equator.

The South Atlantic

On the evening of June 7, my Electra put her wheels down in Africa, the third continent of our journey. That left two more continents before us, Asia and Australia. Also we crossed the equator for the second time since leaving home, the schedule calling for two more crossings beyond India.

It was 3:15 in the morning when we left Parnamirio Airport at Natal, Brazil. The take-off was in darkness. The longer runway, which has lights, was unavailable because a perverse wind blew exactly across it. So I used the secondary runway, whose surface is of grass. In the dark it was difficult even to find it, so Fred and I tramped its length with flashlights to learn what we could and establish something in the way of guiding landmarks, however shadowy.

Withal, we got into the air easily. Once off the ground, a truly pitch dark encompassed us. However, the blackness of the night outside made all the more cheering the subdued lights of my cockpit, glowing on the instruments which showed the way through space as we headed east over the ocean. "The night is long that never finds the day," and our night soon enough was day. I remembered, then, that this was my third dawn in flight over the Atlantic.

The trip was uneventful except for little incidents of long-range flying—just another crossing of this stretch of Atlantic which has been flown so many, many times. Such uneventfulness, I suppose, is a part of expeditioning which comes off successfully. If all goes well, there is not much to report. If all doesn't, there are "incidents."

The weather was exactly as predicted by the efficient Air France meteorologist. Nearly all the way head winds prevailed. I dare say they averaged twenty miles an hour for the first half of the distance. Then came a stretch of doldrums, a period of clear skies, and next an area of low, ragged clouds strewn all about the sky, and the heaviest rain I ever saw. The heavens fairly opened. Tons of water descended, a buffeting weight bearing so heavily on the ship I could almost feel it. Fortunately, that was long after daylight. The water splashed brown against the glass of my cockpit windows, a soiled emulsion mixed with the oil spattering from the propellers.

Our flying speed was about what I had planned. Throughout my flight, calculations had been built on a base speed of 150 miles an hour. Reckoning the distance across the Atlantic as about 1,900 miles, our average fell only little short of the estimate despite head winds. On this stretch, as on those that preceded, I did not at all open up the engines. With plenty of work ahead, I wanted to treat them as gently as could be. When need be we could better our speed twenty or more miles each hour.

About midway we passed an Air France mail plane. Unfortunately I could not "talk" to it. The mail plane's radio equipment, I believe, is telegraphic code, while mine, at the moment, was exclusively voice telephone. As always, I broadcast my position by voice each half hour. Whether it was heard at all, or understood if heard, perhaps I shall never know.

Once before I kept a little diary when flying over the Atlantic, that time on a route some four thousand miles further north. Some of those scribblings later appeared in a book of mine. Here, then, are extracts penciled at random exactly as set down in the "log-book" (which was a loose-leaf stenographer's notebook) while the Electra flew us across the South Atlantic.

6:50 Just crossing equator, 6000 feet. Sun brilliant. Little lamb clouds below. Ahead dark ones.

Ship below. I descend to let him see us for report.

Doldrums. Rain sends clouds. Sperry flies while I do this. Have just come through very heavy rain. Blotted out everything. Looked brown on windshield.

Page from the log book kept on the South Atlantic. It contains the entries that appear on page 74; note the scribble in the left margin, "South Atlantic, Natal St. Louis." It was written when Miss Earhart crossed the equator.

Ragged clouds piled up very high. Giants of S. Atlantic throw liner about carelessly down there. Up here can be rough too. Sky unkempt. Water dirty gray.

Left engine been bumping. Now starts again. Also right. Only too much oil I think.

Gas fumes in plane from fueling made me sick again this morning after starting. Stomach getting weak I guess.

French and Standard oil people very careful about wiping oil cans. No ground wire used as in U.S. In refueling at Natal boys spilled so much gas it was funny. I am charged with 165 gals. in a 149 gal. tank.

Have tried get something on radio. No go. Rain, static. Have never seen such rain. Props a blur in it.

Kinseys sent lunch. Took to field. Odd scene. Frenchmen all rotund. Berets. Champagne bottles along walk. Frenchmen waiting their plane from B. A. not in until 6 A.M.

Rain makes strange patterns on windows. Harried by speed. Indicated our speed 140 at 5780 feet. Man. press. 26½ rpm 1700 5½ hours out.

Driest cockpit ever had . . . boys at Lockheed did a good job. . . . Glad I got that new rubber lining at Fortaleza.

1 hr. 15 mins. doldrums. Seeing nothing but rain now through wispy cloud. Fred dozes. . . . I never seem to get sleepy flying. Often been tired but seldom sleepy.

Outside temp. 60°. Seems to be a cool Equator we've picked—upstairs anyway.

In half hour should be about half way across.

9:41 Natal time. Clouds seem to be changing. Formation seems thinner, shredding out. Rather bright in spots. Can hardly believe sun is north of us but so it is.

147 mph	distance across	1900
8 hrs. out	thus far	1176
1176	"Balance"	724

Posing with more assurance than she felt, Amelia assumes the classic "hands–on–prop" pose.

Three classics: Lockheed Electra, Cord Cabriolet, and Amelia Earhart.

Smithsonian Institution Photo No. 71-1060

The critical moment in the takeoff, when the tail wheel has just left the ground and the rudders are just becoming effective. In Hawaii, the airplane got away from Amelia.

Smithsonian Institution Photo No. 85-14509

Amelia referred to the Electra's cockpit as her "cubbyhole."

Irony. Amelia examines the loop of the Radio Direction Finder unit. Properly installed and properly used, it could have saved her life.

Smithsonian Institution Photo No. 71-1051

Smithsonian Institution Photo No. 74-9260

A complex aircraft for its day, the twin-engine Lockheed had to fly from one primitive airport to another.

Baltimore American

FINAL
PRICE 10 CENTS

The Largest Sunday Circulation in the Entire South

SUNDAY, JULY 4, 1937

EARHART RESCUE PLANES DRIVEN BACK BY STORM; 6 AIR SQUADRONS JOIN HUNT

THRONGS QUIT STEEL PLANT CITY; 8 HURT BY FIREWORKS

Injuries Occur Despite Rigid Police Regulations; Travel Agencies Jammed By Exodus

GUARDED IN BOMB PLOT

Police on Duty at Cambria; Youth Held After Alleged Attempt to Dynamite Train

Missing Pacific Flier And Navigator

AMELIA EARHART AND NAVIGATOR FRED NOONAN

The nation's leading woman flier and the navigator who was helping her in her attempt to fly around the world are shown when they arrived at Venezuela on one of the stages of the flight.

Fears For Two Grow As Gale Sweeps Area

Amelia's Own Story of Hop

By AMELIA EARHART

Gale Lashes Search Area

By WALTER K. NOLAN

Two Flying Boats To Hop Atlantic | **Britain Ready To Fight; Hitler, Duce Warned** | **Amelia Planned For Quiet Life**

By WILLIAM HILLMAN

Spot News Of Sports

RACING

BASEBALL

TENNIS

Mrs. Coolidge Puts $2 In Fireworks

FRANKLIN, ETHEL AT CAMP

THE BALTIMORE NEWS-POST
Will not be published tomorrow—a holiday.

Smithsonian Institution Photo No. A45176

Front-page news in 1937, the disappearance of America's first lady of the air still generates countless theories, but as yet no proof.

Seven hundred and something to go . . . that's about the mileage between Burbank and Albuquerque. Seems long way off . . . long way too from radio beams and lighted airways . . . our flyers at home don't know how pampered they are . . . air lines especially.

High overcast now. Good visibility except now and then showers. Fred takes sight. Says we're north of course a little.

Oil from props and rain on windshield have made smeary emulsion. I cant see through. Nothing to see anyway.

Fred goes back to catch a bug.

That entry ended that particular batch of skywrit recordings. Unexplained it could imply something intimate and embarrassing. Actually what it referred to was remote and scientific.

The creature to be caught was a micro-organism of the upper air. Fred C. Meier of the Department of Agriculture equipped me with a "sky hook" similar to that carried by Colonel Lindbergh in his 1933 Greenland flight. This is a device to obtain in flight samples of air content which are then preserved in sealed aluminum cylinders for microscopic laboratory examination later. The sky hook is, in effect, a metal rod about the length and size of a broomstick in whose end the cylinder is inserted. When extended into the uncontaminated slipstream outside of the plane the cylinder is turned so that the slide within it is exposed to the moving air and gathers upon it whatever minute beasties may inhabit the particular stretch of atmosphere just then being flown through.

We devised a mechanical refinement for our sky hook. Noonan was too busy to hold it extended through either the cockpit window or the door of the fuselage, had either arrangement been practical. So, at Miami, we had brackets fitted to the side of the ship just behind the fuselage door. When this door was open a couple of inches, which was easily done, the device was clamped in these brackets, and the cylinder manually opened. Then for a period of thirty minutes or so nature took its course. Subsequently the cylinder was closed, sealed and the place and time of its exposure recorded.

By the time Africa was reached we had a dozen or more such recordings. In the directions given me, Mr. Meier wrote: "This phase of research was originally opened by Louis Pasteur in classical experiments recorded in 1860 which have since been followed by medical men and botanists of many countries. The results of our new upper air studies bring to light fundamental principles of the spread of microscopic organism by winds. These principles lead to many practical applications, perhaps the most important of which are improved measures of control of diseases of plants and animals."

To get the hang of how to handle them we "exposed" a couple of aluminum cylinders before starting. It happened that Fred coughed upon the slide of one of these.

"That's ruined," he said, starting to throw it away. "The collection of germs on that slide would look like a menagerie under a microscope."

But I insisted on adding that cylinder to our collection. I thought it would give the laboratory workers something unique to ponder when they came upon its contents among the more innocent bacteria of the equatorial upper airs. Heaven knows what cosmic conclusions Fred's contribution might help them reach! . . . Such absurd procedure must be debited to a pilot's perverted sense of humor.

At St. Louis are the headquarters of Air France for the trans-Atlantic service, and I was grateful for the field's excellent facilities,

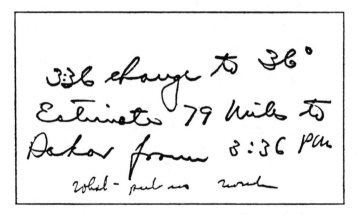

A note that Noonan sent up to A.E. that afternoon crossing the South Atlantic just before they sighted the African coast. At the bottom is her pencil notation, "What put us north?"

which were placed at my disposal. But it is only fair to say that I really had intended to land at Dakar, 163 miles south of St. Louis. The fault was mine.

When we first sighted the African coast, thick haze prevailed and for some time no position sight had been possible. My navigator indicated that we should turn south. Had we done so, a half hour would have brought us to Dakar. But a "left turn" seemed to me in order and after fifty miles of flying along the coast we found ourselves at St. Louis, Senegal. Once arrived above the airport it was wiser to sit down rather than retrace our track over a strange country with the sudden darkness of the tropics imminent. The elapsed time across, by the way, was thirteen hours and twelve minutes.

Dakar

Africa smells. The same smell pervades Dakar as St. Louis. To me it seemed a sort of strong human tang of people, quite different from the aromas of South American cities which are those of fruit, fish, meat and growing things—sometimes overgrown!

(It happens I am one of those people whose sense of smell is acute. Often I recall the odor of flowers, places and people quite as clearly as I can visualize their appearance. In flying such a sense can sometimes be useful, enjoyable, or the reverse. Examples: Detecting the first pungent scent of overly hot oil or rubber—and doing the right thing about it. Quaffing the fragrance of blooming orchards or orange groves, which often carries to considerable altitudes. Recognizing the unmistakable odors which rise from such places as the grassy marshes around Newark or the stockyards of Chicago.)

To get the full impact of fresh scenes, a very good way is to fly into them. To drop down, for instance, out of the western skies upon the coast of Africa. In such an approach the traveler has no period of preparation, of becoming acclimatized, socially and geographically, as must happen on slow steamer voyages with recurrent stops whereon one filters gradually into new environments whose boundaries perforce become imperceptible, their outlines hazy. With an advent like ours the shift of scene was complete, clear-cut. That is the drama of modern air-voyaging. Last week, Home. Yesterday, South America. Today, Africa.

Focused from the kaleidoscopic first impressions, beyond its aromas Africa was to me a riot of human color. An amusing, friendly riot of bright raiment adorning good-natured ebony people. Their clothing contrasted gaudily with the neutral background of brown plains, bare hills, parched vegetation and drab dwellings.

"Feet here are the most interesting thing I have seen." I found that log-book observation written as we hopped over from St. Louis to Dakar.

Probably the superlative was out of order but at that the feet of natives seemed extraordinary. Mostly they wear "toe covers," or no shoes at all. When black feet generously proportioned from generations of heavy-loaded use, were encased in hand-me-down European shoes the results were absurd.

Around the airport at St. Louis stood primitive huts. Tall black figures endowed with a certain innate dignity went about their own affairs without much concern for their neighbor airplanes. Seeing the majesty of these natives I asked myself what many must have asked before: What have we in the United States done to these proud people, so handsome and intelligent in the setting of their own country?

The streets were tropic comic opera. Mother Hubbards draped from native necks. Women carried babies slung haphazardly on their backs or their fronts. They wore headdresses of all types and miraculous conformations and often perched on top were baskets laden with fruit and much beside. Some faces were scarred by tribal slashes. Much of the jewelry could have originated with the American Brass Company, the ladies going in heavily for bracelets and massive necklaces. I saw no disfiguring ornamentation like the nostril buttons worn by some in Paramaribo, which, I am told, were to discourage wife-kissing during husbands' absence from home.

In the cities I heard no native music. Perhaps that is for villages only. Of all God's children who've "got rhythm," few, I dare say, are blessed with it more basically than true Africans.

In the market places there were mountains of peanuts, somewhat held in place by filled sacks. Incidentally, a bag of peanuts very specially fresh roasted was about the only West African export we carried on our way. Subsequently as we munched them Fred and I might have been in the bleachers of a ball-game back home, instead of in the cockpit of a plane spanning remote deserts.

Dakar nestles far out on the peninsula of Cape Verde, the most westerly point of the continent. It is the capital of French West Africa and as a jumping-off point for the South Atlantic holds a commanding position on the route between western Europe and Brazil. The population, I believe, is about 35,000.

On the morning of June 8 we flew the 163 miles from St. Louis. The chief reason I decided to lay over a day at Dakar instead of proceeding east was because my fuelmeter gave out two hours after we left Natal. The very efficient chief mechanic at Dakar discovered that a piece of the shaft was broken. While he worked on that—a difficult job to manage from a blueprint printed in English, which he did not understand, in an aeroplane he did not know—I had a forty-hour check of the engines, probably all they would need until we reached Karachi.

At Dakar again I found my enthusiasm for service given us was rapidly exhausting my supply of superlatives. I wrote to Mr. Putnam asking him to tell Jacques de Sibour how especially helpful everyone had been, and how well the arrangements made by Standard Oil had worked out everywhere.

We were the guests of Monsieur Marcel de Coppet, Governor General, at his spacious mansion. There we had a quiet dinner, followed with a reception by the Aero Club which was the trip's only function up to then. At a meeting of military pilots that afternoon I had to explain that I had only slacks and shirts in which to meet generals, pilots, kings and beggars.

The Governor is a delightfully cultivated person whose gracious hospitality I thoroughly enjoyed. With him especially I was ashamed of my illiteracy. But my French is rudimentary, particularly the aviation brand, which is not taught in school. Instead I remember questions about my uncle's health and my aunt's umbrella, about walking in the "jardin" and shutting the "fenêtre," none of which helps appreciably. With sign language supplemented by scraps of English and French, we contrived to explain what was what without serious trouble. I found that aeronautic fundamentals are international; indeed, I believe that wind cones, indicators of air direction at flying fields, might be adopted as symbols of world understanding.

The French, I have always heard, have a genius for colonization. Certainly they seemed miraculously at home in this particular far corner of the world. I suspect wherever they may be they live well. Where Frenchmen are, there also is good food. Certainly at Natal the meals were delicious, an especially alluring dish being the small reddish fish called "rouget."

Colonel Tavera of the Air Force was generous with information and maps concerning the route easterly, while the Air France officials at St. Louis, Dakar and Natal were extraordinarily helpful. Incidentally, all the advance fuss about passports, permissions, medical certificates and such, apparently was love's labor lost. Up to Dakar no one had asked for a passport. There were no custom examinations, no inspections. About the only formality was signing the police register in St. Louis. Officialdom expected us, knew our plans, and that our papers were in order. So why be troublesome? Altogether an understanding attitude.

The Dakar airport is excellent, picturesquely situated on a jutting point of land with the pink city nearby. I am finishing this account of the flight to date, writing in the hangar while the good mechanics of Air France work. Every inch of the plane has been scrubbed with soap and water. The Electra's periodic face-washings were performed by natives. I must say the aspect of the African grease monkeys was sometimes considerably simian. It was not only oily when we arrived but there was a curious pattern from dust and rain made by the airflow over the wings.

Tomorrow, if all goes well, we start the long air route across Africa. Exactly what course we will fly will be determined as we progress. Extremely hot weather is creating unfavorable conditions in the interior. I am warned of tornadoes to the south and sandstorms on the north. So I must try to squeeze between.

So far our journey has been along established air lanes. From Miami to Natal I followed the regular route of Pan American Airways. From Natal to Dakar we were "in the groove" of the long-established transocean service. Now we turn the nose of the Electra into regions where planes fly frequently but not on schedule.

Central Africa

When I was a little girl in Kansas, the adventures of travel fascinated me. With my sister and my cousins I gratified my ambitions by make-believe. That was in a barn behind our house in Atchison. There, in an old abandoned carriage, we made imaginary journeys full of fabulous perils.

Early we discovered the special joys of geography. The maps of far places that fell into our clutches supplemented the hair-raising experiences of the decrepit carriage. Map-traveling took its place beside window-shopping as an accepted diversion. The map of Africa was a favorite. The very word meant mystery. Blithely we rolled on our tongues such names as Senegal, Timbuctu, Ngami, El Fasher, and Khartoum. We weighed the advantages of the River Niger and the Nile, the comparative ferociousness of the Tauregs and Swahili. No Livingstone, Stanley or Rhodes explored with more enthusiasm than we.

As the girl grew older, the inclination did not mend. Indeed, as flying brought far places closer, the horizon, and what lay beyond it, gained added lure.

More than once the Electra's pilot, who had been that little girl, thought of those early flights of fancy in the old carriage as she herself flew almost straight across Central Africa from the Atlantic to the Red Sea. For me the dreams of long ago had come true. Only, back in Atchison, our imaginary African treks were on camels or elephants. Then airplanes were of another day.

Weather reports at the Dakar air field were not altogether

encouraging. There were barometric lows threatening tornadoes, or their local equivalent, in the Sudanese region through which our route lay. So, instead of going to Niamey as at first planned, on the advice of Colonel Tabera, I decided to shift the course slightly to the north, making our objective Gao on the upper reaches of the River Niger. Just before six o'clock we were in the air and seven hours and fifty minutes later came down at Gao in the French Sudan.

Our course from the coast inland over the Senegal and Niger districts lay almost exactly due east. Loafing along at a trifle under 150 miles an hour, the 1,140 mile journey ended pleasantly in the early afternoon. A third of the way we crossed the River Senegal, and four hundred miles further the scattered lakes and upper reaches of the Niger River with a hilly country to our right. North, perhaps within sight had we known where and when to look, was fabled Timbuctu, four hundred miles up the river from Gao.

This outpost of the Sahara has a population of about five thousand. Once it was an important city, political center of the western Sudan, which the French have occupied since 1900. Scanty ruins of ancient Gao remain, chief among them a truncated pyramid and what is left of the tomb of Mohammed Askia and a great mosque, dating back to the seventh or eighth century.

Gao is the terminus of the trans-Saharan motor traffic from the north, a transport of increasing importance. From the city southward the Niger is navigable for over one thousand miles until it empties with many mouths into the Gulf of Guinea, where the name "Slave Coast" is reminder of unsavory activities of not so many years ago.

In our hasty visit, the beginning and the end of Gao for us was the airport. We wanted the keys of no city so long as the hangar doors were open and the ground crew ready. Always they were and it was. And always we found my usual calling cards, fifty-gallon drums of gasoline, each with my name printed large upon it in white or red lettering. The exact quantity of fuel, all as arranged months before, waited at each stopping place and additionally at many which changed schedules or leap-frogging eliminated. The first thing we were apt to see as we rolled into any hangar from Caripito to Port Darwin was an orderly group of these "Amelia Earhart" drums, their contents waiting to be consumed by the thirsty Electra. The metal barrels, empty, were left behind as souvenirs.

85

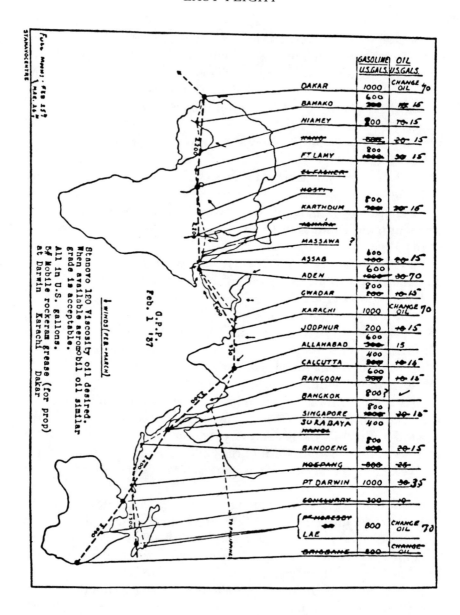

Chart, used in the preparation of the trip, designating the amount of gasoline and oil spotted at each landing place. The revisions in quantity were made when the route was reversed from east-west to west-east.

As usual, our arising at Gao was before dawn, a start made notable by a marvelous breakfast, whose chef d'oeuvre was a mushroom omelet supplemented with cups of fine French chocolate. Thence our revised route took us to Fort Lamy about a thousand miles away. This central Africa is a land of generous distances. Thousand mile hops seem routine. One quickly becomes accustomed to the feeling that when places are separated by a paltry five hundred miles they may be considered practically neighbors, aeronautically speaking. As a matter of fact at this stage we did no very long long-distance hopping. But even so, four separate flights accounted for 4,350 miles. That means a daily stint of about the distance from New York to St. Louis which, cumulatively, without replacement of ship or pilot, is a strenuous schedule, especially if it be but a part of a program with a prologue and an aftermath.

On this day's flying to Lamy and the next, we crossed stretches of country barren beyond words, a no-man's land of eternal want, where the natives cling tenaciously to an existence almost incomprehensible to westerners. First we followed down the Niger River one hundred and seventy miles, checking over the military post at Niamey. Later I learned that French authorities were at the field to receive us. In retrospect I was sorry that I did not drop down to pay a call. But at the time, with the weather treating us well, it seemed wise to press on.

Much of the terrain of that portion of Central Africa over which we flew is remarkably like the southwestern part of the United States. So much so that often it was almost necessary to pinch myself to realize how far from Arizona and New Mexico I actually had strayed. It is, of course, a hot country, with broad stretches of arid desert land, hemmed by regions rough and mountainous. And all beautiful. For from the air the broad views, of whatever country, ever changing, ever shifting in coloring, light and shadow hold beauty which only the willfully blind could ignore.

The difference between this part of Africa that I saw and our own "badland" country lies principally in what humans have accomplished. In these wild lands highways appeared entirely lacking. The roads were mostly trails, crookedly wandering far and wide. And, of course, there were few of those welcome emergency landing fields of our own West, and no aviation luxuries like radio beams and lights. But at that I sometimes felt that the names on the map might just as well have read "Albuquerque" and "Yuma" instead of "El Birni" and "Abu Zabbad."

From a flyer's standpoint, the cross-Africa route, given good weather, is not a difficult one. For much of the way level places for emergency landing are easy to find. There are excellent natural airports and creditable service even including first-rate weather forecasting. In addition to military flying—the French and British have much equipment stationed throughout northern Africa—there is considerable transport aviation. A definite airway stretches eastward from Dakar to Khartoum, where it joins the Cape to Cairo route.

But with all that has been done, maps for the most part are far from satisfactory. This desert mid-region is a difficult country, and years of work will be required to map it well. We had the best maps available, supplemented with information from pilots at each stop. But even so, it was not easy going where we had to depend upon them.

Normally over land one utilizes contact flying, by which is meant following a map with landmarks spotted below. But in a strange country a periodic check of position by celestial navigation can be comforting. In Fred Noonan's judgment finding one's way over Africa was more difficult than over oceans.*

Aviation has come to loom large in the life of these remote posts. In years gone by it took weeks and months to get from one to another, or to the railroads that led to civilization. Mostly such travel was by camel. Now a couple of days' flying can link almost any isolated community with the outer world.

While familiarity with aviation has bred enthusiasm among the personnel which is served by wings, if there is no contempt at least there is no wonder about airplanes in the eyes of the natives. Once the miraculous man-made birds filled them with awe. Today, large-

---

*"From a navigational aspect our flights over the desert were more difficult than over water," subsequently he wrote home from Massawa. "That was because the maps of the country are very inaccurate and consequently extremely misleading. In fact, at points no dependence at all could be placed on them. Also recognizable landmarks are few and far between, one part of the desert being as much like another as two peas in a pod. However, we were lucky in always reaching our objectives. In all the distance I don't think we wandered off the course for half an hour, although there were times when I wouldn't have bet a nickel on the accuracy of our assumed position." About a month before departure, Fred Noonan married Mary Beatrice Martinelli of Oakland. To his wife he sent frequent letters or messages.

GOUVERNEMENT GÉNÉRAL
—
L'AFRIQUE OCCIDENTALE FRANÇAISE.

SERVICE MÉTÉOROLOGIQUE

Nº _____ MET

RENSEIGNEMENTS MÉTÉOROLOGIQUES

pour le trajet aérien
de _____ _____
fournis le _____ _____
par la station météorologique
de _____

STATION de _____

ALTITUDE : _____

Fiche rédigée par M _____

PRÉVISION valable jusqu'au _____
(La hauteur de la base des nuages est exprimée dans les prévisions au-dessus du niveau de la mer)

Vent au sol : _____

Vent _____

État du ciel : _____

Visibilité : _____

Remarques : _____

VENT EN ALTITUDE

OBSERVATIONS DE LA ROUTE

_____ le _____ : coucher du soleil à _____ h. ; lever du soleil à _____ h. Rouge phénomènes dangereux.
Les heures sont indiquées en T. M. G.

This sheet is typical of the weather reports supplied Miss Earhart through mid-Africa. This one was made at Dakar covering the region to Niamey for the 10th of June. Miss Earhart's penciled notation "Save" appears in the upper left hand corner.

ly, they are accepted as being almost as commonplace as camels or tractors. In my study at home hangs a cartoon that tells the story. A blasé and technically informed African native with spear and shield regards a plane winging overhead. Says he: "H'm, a new Lockheed!"

From Zinder the land below our air trail dropped into the broad valley of the Yobe River, the largest western affluent of Lake Chad. Long arms and bayous of brown water backed up across the land. Later I learned that all of this had once been a part of the lake itself, whose boundaries, in the very flat country which surrounds much of it, are amazingly elastic. Unusual rains will spread its area unbelievably.

Lake Chad lies almost exactly half way across the continent, a huge shallow body of water which sprawls over some 30,000 square miles. As we saw it from the air, Chad has no distinguishable shorelines. For miles back from the open water were indeterminate swampy regions as much lake as land. Islands of many sizes and fantastic shapes, some of grass actually afloat, lay outlined darkly against the paler water.

Looking down on these islands I glimpsed pictures of strange creatures and outlandish Things, with lumpy paws, flat heads and ghoulish abnormalities. My mind flashed back to our departure from Newfoundland nine years ago when queerly shaped lakes depicted gigantic footprints, a buffalo, a prehistoric animal, so clearly that I set down sketches of some of them in my notebook. That time the pictures were made by water against land. Now it was land against water.

Fleeting as such impressions were (a pilot has little time for scenery, however entertaining) one Grotesque remained clear in mind. It was a Goop—unmistakably a sprawling, ugly Goop somehow strayed to the Sudan. You remember, of course, George Adolphus, the Goop who made his mother cry?

> The Goops they gug and gumble,
> They spill their broth
> On the tablecloth,
> They lead disgusting lives.

A vagrant memory that, of flight over Africa.

This watery region offers a happy feeding ground for cranes and maribou storks whose business in life is scooping up fish with their bills. Blue herons also are plentiful. Birds in great numbers we saw below us but seldom close enough to be recognizable.

While I was told that game abounds, we saw none of the much-advertised elephants, or even crocodiles. But then, a pilot busy with the hundred and one gadgets of her cockpit has little time for game seeking. A landing field located where one expects to find it is quite as exciting a sight as any herd of giant tuskers. At that, we did glimpse a considerable number of hippopotami, who seemed to resent our presence mildly.

Mostly, though, we were flying high, or visibility was impeded by haze which rose almost like steam from the sweltering lands beneath, so our opportunities for intimate sightseeing were limited. The villages have a character all their own. Their formations were curiously irregular. Nowhere were they laid out in squares, and such as we passed over were, for the most part, colorless.

Between times at stopping places I was able to see a little of some of these habitations near the airports. Mostly the natives live in huts that look like bee-hives, made from dried millet stalks. Incidentally, this is a land of opposites. One writes from right to left, takes off one's shoes and leaves one's hat on when entering the house. In land transport one travels by night and sleeps by day. And in constructing these huts, the roof goes on first and the rest is build downward.

About the villages the women do the work. Killing time appears to be the chief occupation of the males. Wives, I am told, are plural. If the husbands are prosperous, very plural.

Children are carried on the mother's back. There is a fine technique in getting them there. The youngster is caught by the wrist and adroitly swung up on mamma's shoulders, legs on either side of her waist, and there tied in place, encompassed in a piece of clothing with arms inside and head alone sticking out. As the infant's hands are not free, it has no way to dislodge the flies that gather on its face, particularly about its eyes. The stolid patience of the youngsters is amazing, the flies usually having a field day before they whimper. If and when baby does make a fuss, mother throws the end of the "tobe" over the child's head and waggles him to sleep.

Many boys and girls have tribal marks cut in their cheeks. I was told that salt is rubbed in to keep the slits open. The little girls wear a short skirt made of strips of leather hung from the belt, which swings like a kilt when they walk. If there is enough cotton cloth to go around, the boys are adorned with a single garment—a large sack-like shirt with holes for the arms. Otherwise their birthday suits suffice.

Wells, of course, are the beginning and the end of desert villages. Where there is water there are habitations. When the well dries the village moves. Speaking of water, to the east of Chad is a strange phenomenon. Throughout that region the tebeldi tree is used as a water reservoir. Natives scoop out the inside of the trunk, which can be done without killing the tree, thereby making a tank which may hold from 500 to 1,000 gallons of water. This is doled out through a spigot that is plugged into the tree at lowering heights as the water supply diminishes, and is borne away in leather buckets for individual use. Under such circumstances bathing ranks far down the list of necessities.

To the Red Sea

Daybreak starts had been the order of our going because it was wise to get flying finished by noon when possible. Normally, the greatest heat came after midday, to be avoided both by man and machine. Not that either Fred or I particularly minded the occasional broiling of cockpit or fuselage (often the outer coating of the plane's metal was too hot to touch, while the temperatures of its innards sometimes were so high for our peace of mind we avoided recording them). But very hot air can make difficult flying. It is thin and lacks lifting power. On equatorial fields, with the sun reflecting from the sands, one has to watch landing speed, which must be faster than normal. Also after a day of heat the air is apt to be particularly rough.

Despite our plans we were held until half past one in the afternoon at Fort Lamy. That was because of a small leak in a shock absorber of the landing gear. Air from one oleo escaped. To pump it up again taxed the manpower resources of the little station almost to capacity. There are more pleasant diversions than hand-pumping at a temperature well over one hundred degrees.

Because of the late start we made the objective of that day's flight El Fasher, in French Equatorial Africa. With a following wind we negotiated the journey in something over three hours. As expected, thanks to the day's heat, which caught up to us, it was particularly bumpy flying, with a particularly desolate region below us.

Because of detailed information given me, I was on the lookout for the "eight foot thorn hedge" surrounding El Fasher's airport, which hurdle, coming and going, we successfully negotiated. Its purpose is not so much to herd planes within as to keep animals without. The airdrome itself was a splendid natural landing field, though with few facilities. There we were met by Governor and Mrs. P. Ingallson of Darfur Province, who took the wayfarers to their home, once a Sultan's palace, where my room was next door to the harem of other days.

Here again I was impressed with the gracious informality of officialdom in the field. All this African crossing had been pictured to us as "difficult" from the standpoint of red tape. But once arrived on the ground, formalities were forgotten. All concerned did their utmost to make matters easy for a properly accredited flyer, even of the feminine gender—or, perhaps, for all I know, especially of that gender. Even the unavoidable disinfecting on landing seemed to irk those who conducted it far more than the disinfectees. It would be impossible for flit guns to be handled with greater grace and discretion than were those directed on us. Everything within the plane was squirted with germ-destroying vapor. Our personal luggage being infinitesimal and our cargo nil, the operation did not offer much of a problem—there just wasn't sustenance for self-respecting bacteria.

After a night at El Fasher we flew further into Anglo Egyptian Sudan, on the morning of Sunday, June 13th. The map of the region around El Fasher and eastward holds more and larger blanks than that of any other territory we traversed. On it El Fasher is the one metropolis of sorts with miles of dotted red lines (which, according to the map's legend, are native tracks) and a limited number (five to be exact) of "cleared roads fit for motor traffic" burgeoning out from it. West of the town is a hilly country wherein the map optimistically indicates various rivers (being the dry season, we saw none) which start bravely but after an inch or two (on the map) end in the oblivion of the thirsty sands.

Back in California such maps covering the entire journey had been meticulously prepared. On them the routes to be followed, and often alternate routes, were drawn in, with the compass courses in both directions. The distances between landmarks, and between airdromes, were marked, as well as major elevations of the terrain. Every landing field was shown by an inked-in circle easy for a pilot's eye to locate. They were, I think, thoroughly practical.

East of El Fasher our route crossed a cartographical blank space as large as an outstretched hand with not a contour line on it or a river or the name even of a "village of the sixth grade," than which, one imagines, there can be few hamlets more lowly. Five hundred miles separate El Fasher from Khartoum. The first half is utterly flat, arid, uninhabited, and lacks landmarks altogether, at least for the uninitiated. That dreary locality is labeled "Dabbat el Asala."

It would be fun at leisure to explore these maps even without ever visiting the territory they concern. Text in the upper left corner of one records that: "In the bed of the Wadi Howar two heglig trees about four hundred meters apart were ringbarked. They mark the intersection of the twenty-fourth meridian." Other notations sprawled about the wide open spaces include the following: "Rolling desert no trees"; "Many remains of animals"; "High level plateau with scanty grass, some bush, stony"; "Swamp in rain, salt pan"; "Standing water until Nov."; "Wells. Water never entirely fails";

KHARTOUM
(Sudan)

LAT. 15° 35' N.   1 mile E. of railway station.
LONG. 32° 34' E.   SIZE 2,700' × 1,950'.   ALTITUDE 1,250'.

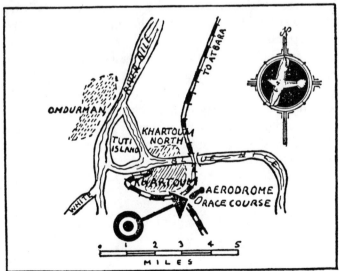

"Large rahad and grazing ground." There are, too, such priceless names as Qala-en Hahl, Umm Shinayshin, Abu Seid, Idd el Bashir, Fazi, Marabia Abu Fas. Such offer fine stimulus for geographical cross-word puzzlers.

On my lap as we approached Khartoum, clipped to the larger map on which the compass course was laid out, was a detailed drawing of the city's airports in relation to their environment. Facts about the local situation stared me in the face. As, for instance: "Dimensions 2,700 × 1,950 ft. Surface, sand and cotton soil, soft after rain. Landmarks, junction of Blue and White Nile, town and racecourse. Remarks, landing in the area near racecourse should be avoided after rain."

How many months had passed since the last rain I did not know, and no one seemed concerned about the next. Heat waves danced up from the surface of the desert. The temperature was 110 degrees in the shade. If there was any softness about the field, it came from dust, not mud.

Khartoum is the capital of Anglo Egyptian Sudan, situated beside the Nile 1,350 miles south of Cairo, with which it is connected by rail and steamer. Since leaving Fortaleza in Brazil it was our most considerable metropolis, with a population of about 50,000.

Seen from the air one was struck by the symmetry with which the city is laid out. I failed to realize it at the time, but was later told the squares and streets form the design of the Union Jack. It was Kitchener who drew the plan for the city in 1898, after his troop took it from the successor to the Mahdi, who had besieged and killed Gordon at Khartoum in 1885. Names and deeds great in the military history of England are interwoven with the story of this region. And beside it flows the Nile, "asleep in lap of legends old." Seeing this cradle-land of history for the first time and having come so far one could weep to pass so briefly, not lingering,

> To eat the lotus of the Nile
> And drink the poppies of Cathay.

Two hours in Khartoum!

So . . . we refueled, and paid our respects to the cordial British officials whose language sounded so very pleasant in our ears. That done, and our bill for £3 22s. landing fee settled, we were on our way again toward Massawa in Italy's Eritrea on the eastern edge of Africa.

The hop from Khartoum was as interesting as any part of the trip. The country, except that near the Nile, was bleak desert for many miles. Only a few caravan trails were visible, and now and then a camp with a tent or two in the midst of the stretching sand. I could see fine lines on the surface, whether from camel trails or wind streaks I do not know. Possibly only wrinkles in the ancient face of the wasteland.

Exactly two hundred miles out we crossed at right angles at Atbara River which flows northward into the Nile. Thence the low desert roughened and rose, first into sloping sandy foothills, then mountains where green vegetation, almost the first we had seen in Africa, began to appear below us. Well into Eritrea we flew over the headwaters of a second considerable river, the Khor Baruka, which drains this highland region northward into the Red Sea. Heated air blasted up from the mountain slopes, buffeting the ship unkindly. Even above 10,000 feet it was rough going.

We flew not far from Asmara, 7,000 feet high, Eritrea's capital. To its comparative coolness come those who can escape from the furnace of Massawa in the summer months. Later I learned that on this Hamasien plateau is being constructed a large new airport. It is named for Colonel Umberto Maddalena, who accompanied Air Marshal Balbo on the mass flight across the Atlantic to Brazil in 1931. I had hoped that by some happy chance General Balbo himself might be "in these parts." My last memory of that colorful soldier (whose beard so strikingly resembles the adornment of that other great flyer, our good friend Sir Hubert Wilkins) concerns a ride he gave me in a low-slung racing car from Rome to Ostia. He elected to show the woman pilot something about speed on the ground. He did!

To our right neighboring peaks reared to perhaps 14,000 feet as the range reached southward into Abyssinia. As the visibility was good doubtless we looked over onto that forbidden territory. While the Italian authorities had been gracious in granting permissions as regarded Eritrea, foreign flying over Abyssinia itself is discouraged.

The mountains over which we flew gained their crest of about 10,000 feet only thirty miles from salt water and our destination.

&. C. Form No. 1L.   مطبوع ج۰س۰ نمرة ۱۱

SUDAN CUSTOMS
جمارك السودان

PERMIT TO DEPART. اذن سفر. № 9979 نمرة

Port of _____ Khartoum Aerodrome _____ اسم الميناء

S. S. _____ Aircraft N.R. 16020 _____ اسم المركب

Nationality _____ USA _____ جنسيه

Master _____ Miss Earhart. _____ اسم الرئيس

Nature of Cargo _____ nil _____ نوع الشحنة

Destination _____ Massawa _____ الجهة المقصودة

Date of Clearance _____ 13·1·37 _____ تاريخ التخليص

Customs Stamp. ختم الجمرك

Place _____ Khartoum _____ الجهة

Date _____ 13·1·37 _____ التاريخ

Chief Customs Officer رئيس الجمرك

(MoC. 7479) S. G. 983 G. 100 Bks. 9/35.

Our slide down those abrupt eastern slopes was, perforce, no straight coasting, but the way of a snake. I had to spiral down.

From the heights we saw the Red Sea. It is not red, but blue. (Both the Blue and the White Nile were green.) Beyond it we sighted a shimmering land of mirages that was Arabia. Across it, or around it, our course lay from the blue Red Sea to Karachi, India, a jump as long as spanning the Atlantic.

The airport at Massawa was of ample size with large hangars. While I do not speak a word of Italian, and it was some time after our arrival before anyone could be found who understood English, yet in short order mechanics were at work changing the oil, checking spark-plugs and the like.

Massawa admits to being one of the hottest cities in the world. In the summer the thermometer often hits 120 degrees in the shade. For a typical July the mean temperature was 94, twenty degress hotter than the average for the hottest month in New York—truly a mean temperature! On the evening of our arrival the thermometer registered 100 degrees, but that night it became comparatively cool. Our hosts assured us, however, that as yet the season was too early to be truly hot. The later summer months apparently provide the town's torrid reputation.

Massawa has a population of about 15,000 natives and a few hundred Europeans beside the military. It stands at the north end of a broad bay, built partly on one larger and two smaller coral islands, and the neighboring mainland. The fine harbor lies within the islands where we saw the local nondescript sailing craft called "sambuks," and a couple of "baby clippers," miniature square-rigged ships built of teakwood. By chance I learned that such a pocket size "square-rigger" recently acquired in Ceylon by our friends the W. A. Robinsons was anchored in Aden as I passed over a day later.

Mostly visiting vessels are freighters, come to Massawa for salt. As we flew down into the evening shadows I saw beside the town great gleaming heaps which I thought to be white sand-dunes. Instead they were huge piles of salt. The blistering sun is Massawa's potent manufacturer. It draws off countless gallons of water daily, leaving behind thick coatings of salt in the shallow evaporating pans whence barefoot natives gather up the crystal crop, much of it destined for shipment to Japan.

We were lodged that night in Italian army quarters, guests of Colonel De Silvestro Luigi, in command, acting for General Laghi. The neat apartment houses were as clean as could be, each room with bed, chair, table, and portable closet. Electric lights, a fan, and a little ice-box for keeping the water cool were luxuries that would delight any housekeeper.

It had been a long day, what with the landmarkless desert flying, the stop at Khartoum, the rough going over the mountains and the long trip down, and there was fair reason for a pilot to feel famished. (As usual I had forgotten to eat.)

"Are you hungry?" an English-speaking officer asked me.

"As hollow as a bamboo horse." It took ingenuity to translate into appropriate Italian that implausible simile, a standby of childhood days.

Arabian Flight

On Tuesday, June 14, we moved down the Red Sea from Massawa to Assab to prepare for the long flight along the Arabian coast to India. Assab was nearer our objective than Massawa, offered better take-off facilities, and as well we had a greater supply of 87 Octane gasoline spotted there.

Eritrea stretches along the coast of the Red Sea for 670 miles. Our course took us about half that length. Soon we left behind the mountains that bordered the coast-line and bade farewell to everything that was green. Approaching Assab the coast became torridly barren beyond description. It was at Assab that Italy gained first foothold in what is now Eritrea, when an Italian steamship company in 1870 purchased land there for a coaling station. From that beginning Italian influence expanded northward, carving out the Eritrea of today, which in the last few years became the military spring-board for the conquest of Abyssinia. Most of the troop movements for that operation were through Massawa.

Incidentally, in a phone talk from India to New York (of which more anon) I later learned that our departure from Massawa had been announced as an actual take-off for Karachi. When we became long overdue at that Indian destination naturally there was anxiety regarding us. All the while in reality we were sitting at Assab. Communication thence to London and Paris sometimes requires a full

٢٦ فبراير سنة ١٩٣٧

الآنسة اميليا ابرهارت
رحلة لضرب الرقم القياسي للطيران حول العالم
——

اعضاء الرحلة • الآنسة اميليا ابرهارت بوتنام قائدة الطائرة —
هارى مانج مساعد
جاك دى سبور (ربما من كراتشي الى دكار)

الطائــــــرة • بمحركين ماركة • لوكهيد الكترا مركب عليهما سائق اوتوماتيكي وآلة راديو
تشتغل تلغرافيا وصوتيا •

علامات التسجيل• ن • ر • ١٦٠٢٠

لون الطائـرة • فضي

المحركات • اثنان • هـ • واسب قوة كل منهما ٥٥٠ حصانا • هذان المحركان اكبر
من المحركات المركبة بالطائرات العادية • ويمكن للطائرة ان تستمر في الجو
بمحرك واحد مع حمولة عادية •

الحمولة المقررة • ١٠٥٠٠ رطل

مدة الطيران • الفين مــيـــل

مجموع سمة الخزانات• ١١٥٠ جالون اميكاني (بنزين)
اكبر كمية يمكن اخذها)
للطيران خارج منطقة } ٧٠٠ جالون اميكاني
المحيط الباسفيكي {

استهلاك البنزين • كل ساعة طيران عادى ٣١٠ رطل بالوزن

وقد طعّم اعضاء الرحلة ضد الحمى التيفودية والجدرى وهم يحملون شهادات
تقرر عدم احـرازهم سلحة نارية او آلات سينمترافية • وهؤلاء الاعضاء انكليز يتمتعون بحماية
حضرة صاحب الجلالة الامبراطورى الملك والامبراطور جرج السادس وهم ذاهبون في مهمة خصوصية
من كراتشي الى عــدن !

●●●●●●●●●●●●●●●●●●●●

Arabic credentials.

day. Apparently we had actually departed from Assab before New York knew we even had arrived there.

At this sweltering outpost of Italian authority on the Red Sea the same cordial hospitality extended to us at Massawa was renewed. With the group of officers and flyers there under Teniente Colonel Rinaldo Neri we had the pleasantest possible, though abbreviated, visit.

We left Assab early on the morning of the fifteenth, well before daylight. First we cut across a deep indentation on the Eritrean coast, and thence at an angle flew over the narrow southern entrance to the Red Sea called Bab-al-Mandah to the Arabian shore. That reached, we straightened out over the desolate southeastern tip of Arabia, checking over Aden after the sun was well up, one hundred and seventy-five miles on our way.

Flying by foreigners over Arabia is not welcomed. In the early stages of planning our journey a course was advised eliminating the straight trans-Arabian hop between mid-Africa and Karachi. For a time it seemed I might have to go around north by Cairo and Bagdad, and down through Persia on the normal Europe–Australia air route. That detour would have added perhaps another two thousand miles of flying and made a considerable jog north of the approximate equatorial route.

Finally the authorities relented. They concluded, I believe, that my plane was capable of making the two thousand mile nonstop flight necessary to carry it from the Red Sea to India, without undue likelihood of forced landing on Arabia's forbidden sands. The British were very friendly and co-operative about it. They gave permission to land at Aden, and permission to fly thence to Karachi, possibly stopping first at Gwadar, 350 miles up the coast at the mouth of the Persian Gulf in Baluchistan close to the Persian border. It was stipulated that we were not to fly over Arabia itself but along the edge of the sea.

I understood that unfavorable winds might make the field at Aden difficult for heavy take-off, and so took on a full load of fuel at Assab, deciding to push through at least to Gwadar, and perhaps to Karachi if all went well and daylight lasted long enough.

So from Aden, as directed, I held a course along the coast. Sometimes the blue Arabian Sea was below. Sometimes clouds piled along the ocean's edge forced us shoreward for brief stages. Flying high, we were able to see considerable of this forbidden and forbidding country.

Surely some of the wastelands of the world bordered our route. One could scarcely imagine a more desolate region than that shore, although on the first third of the journey a few villages appeared along the water front, wedged in between mountains and sea. Such a one was Makalle, a metropolis of that portion of Hadramaut, which is the southern region of Arabia. Behind the mountains the map shows the interior an almost unbroken sandy desert. Where rough mountains did not wet their feet in the sea, low sandhills rolled down to the water's edge. Inland we could see the tips of tilted hills and dry river canyons. Some regions looked as if mighty harrows had churned the tortured badlands into a welter of razor-back ridges, fantastic mountains and thirsty valleys barren of vegetation and devoid of life. Surprisingly here and there in this desolation a number of emergency flying fields appeared.

In no part of southern Arabia is a forced landing desirable. The waterless, treeless desert geography is in itself pretty hopeless, a further negative factor being the probable attitude of the sparse nomadic population, if, as, and when encountered. In some districts the Arab tribesmen might not be hospitable to strange interlopers, especially a woman. Or perhaps under special circumstances too hospitable.

I know the officials concerned did not relish such possibilities, however remote. Indeed, neither did we. But the Electra and my Wasp engines never had failed me, and I felt they would carry on so long as fuel lasted.

Anyway, as a special precaution we carried a letter written in Arabic, presumably addressed "To Whom It May Concern" and bespeaking for us those things which should be bespoken. At least I think so. We had it translated by two people in New York. One linguist, allegedly familiar with things Arabic, said it would be just too bad for us if such an introduction was presented to the wrong local faction. His counsel left me a trifle confused. We carried the document anyway, tucked beside me in the cockpit, ready for emergency. We carried, too, a pretty generous supply of water in canteens, concentrated foods, a small land compass, and very heavy walking shoes. Fortunately we did not have to walk!

Beyond Ras el Hadd, which is on the eastern end of Arabia, facing the Gulf of Oman, we cut across to Gwada, which we checked over at five o'clock. Thence we skirted the coast southeastward to Karachi, arriving at 7:05 P.M.

I think our elapsed time for the 1,920 miles from Assab to Karachi was 13 hours and 10 minutes. Perhaps we could have done better if my manual mixture-control lever had not jammed. With it misbehaving, I could not regulate the quantity of fuel consumed by the right engine, which gulped gasoline unconscionably. I was afraid I should run out of fuel, so I reduced the speed to economize.

In Karachi I was told that a nonstop flight from the Red Sea to India had not previously been made. Certainly with or without stops it is no hackneyed route. For me, who had never flown outside of North America (excepting a couple of oceans) this bit of far-away air adventuring was a deeply interesting experience.

One of the customs I had become used to was being fumigated. Every time the plane landed, attendants with flit guns or more elaborate contraptions flung open the door and began squirting. Having been in a yellow fever district, Fred and I were suspects, warnings of our coming having been sent on ahead. However, a rumor which apparently found some circulation at home, to the effect that we might be quarantined in India for nine days, had no foundation. Our robust healthfulness appeared beyond question once the British medical authorities had at us.

The first person to greet us at Karachi was Jacques de Sibour. Perversely I may introduce him as the husband of Violette, the charming American-born daughter of Gordon Selfridge of London who for years has winged around Europe, Africa and Asia with her pilot-husband. Beyond that, de Sibour was the good fairy of our flight. It was he who gathered together the maps and helpful data, arranged supplies and generally made a journey around the world as easy as such a journey possibly could be.

"There's a phone call for you," he said after our greetings.

"Oh, yes." My interest was mild. Probably a local newspaper.

Jacques persisted. "From New York. G. P. on the wire."

As casual as that! And we almost exactly on the other side of the world.

Here is that telephone conversation* as it occurred later that day after the far-flung business of arranging the "connection" had been worked out.

"How do you feel?"

"Swell! Never better."

"How's the ship?"

"Everything seems okeh. There's been a little trouble with the fuel flow-meter and analyzer but I think they'll cure that here."

"How long will you stay in Karachi?"

"Probably two days. I want everything checked thoroughly. Wednesday, with luck, we'll shove off."

"Where to?"

"Probably Calcutta."

"How about this report you're going to be quarantined?"

"I don't think so. Everyone is being most awfully nice to us."

"How's Fred?"

"Fine."

"Are you the first person to fly from the Red Sea across Arabia to Karachi?"

"I hadn't thought of that. I'll try to let you know. [Pause.] Jacques de Sibour is here and he says he thinks this is the first nonstop flight across to India. It was fun."

"Having a good time?"

"You betja! It's a grand trip. We'll do it again, together, some time."

"O.K. with me. Anything else?"

"Well, I'll cable tomorrow an estimate of when we should get to Howland. Good-bye. . . . See you in Oakland."

---

*It was recorded mechanically in the office of the *Herald Tribune* in New York. The conversation traveled 8,274 miles. From Karachi to Bombay, communication was by land lines; from Bombay to London, and thence to New York, by short-wave radio.

Later there were other long long-distance conversations, from Calcutta and Bandoeng and Soerabaga, the latter two routed across the Pacific, covering about 12,000 miles. For the last, G.P.P., en route to California by United plane, was picked up at Cheyenne, Wyoming, his back-of-the-world chat being sandwiched into a twenty minute refueling stop there.

The last conversation, with both voices clearly recorded, ended:

G.P.P—"Is everything about the ship O.K. now?"

A. E.—"Yes. Good night, Hon."

G.P.P.—"Good night. . . . I'll be sitting in Oakland waiting for you."

Karachi

Alluring opportunities to linger along the way cropped up recurrently. At Karachi, for instance, I received an invitation from the Maharaja of Jodhphur to land at his private airport three hundred miles southward. The Maharaja's country is noted for its attractions, and he for boundless hospitality. But, alas, that was a digression to be catalogued for another day.

On my first morning in India I had a small adventure riding a camel. I saw one with particularly gay trappings along the airport road, obviously for hire. His master's costume was in keeping. Over very full trousers he wore a shiny black alpaca coat, pleated to the waist at the back. From under this the tail of his shirt protruded. He had on a rather high turban, and hid most of his facial expressions behind a bushy beard.

The owner explained that his camel was a naughty one. I wanted to tell him I should be naughty, too, if I had two leather plugs in my nose to which guiding reins were attached, but I could not get that idea across. Apparently bits are never used.

Whatever his disposition, my hired steed knelt down and I climbed into the saddle swung between his two humps. It was a startling take-off as we rose. A camel unhinges himself in most extraordinary fashion. As his hind legs unfold you are threatened with a nose-dive forward. Then with a lurch that can unhorse (I mean uncamel) the unwary, the animal's center section, so to speak, hoists into the air. It is reminiscent of the first symptoms of a flat spin. Camels should have shock absorbers.

"Better wear your parachute," Fred shouted.

Later, four of us tried cameling again, visiting a so-called oasis a few miles outside the city. There were many "ships of the desert" careening along the roads loaded far beyond their mammalian Plymsol lines with everything from vegetables to human beings. The latter, like the roving wine merchants in Rome, are often sound asleep. Their stately beasts swing along on their sponge pads, superciliously confident that men still cannot get on without them in some localities.

I visited the post-office to get the "covers" I was carrying canceled. The Director of Post and Telegraph and the postmaster were very courteous and co-operative, permitting me to select the stamp I wished used. Of course, I chose the Karachi airmail type, which, I hoped, would look well on the already decorated envelopes. I was shown behind the scenes at the post-office and watched money orders being made out in rupees—a coin out of books to me. Near by, turbaned postmen sorted mail. Karachi is an important airmail center and will soon become more so as schedules and connections are bettered by air lines around the world.

So far the service in pre-arranged supplies had been unconditionally perfect. Here a large box from Pratt & Whitney of Hartford, Connecticut, containing engine "spares" awaited us. Up to Karachi we had encountered no major mechanical troubles. But little things were hard to get. Differences in size of the threads of screws, for instance, made substitutions impossible. Perhaps aviation will force international agreement in engineering detail as well as in other things.

Every time I drove past the airport I noticed signs warning the public to keep away. In contrast to the United States, there seemed to be no parking place for cars. No attempt was made to "sell" aviation to the passing public. Every facility is put at the flyer's disposal, however. Imperial Airways mechanics worked all day checking my plane, and Group Captain Henderson of the Royal Air Force sent two of his expert instrument men to make whatever adjustments I might need.

Landward from Karachi there is desert. To the north is the thirsty hilly landscape of Kohistan, the limestone spurs of the Kirthir range, breaking down southwards into sandy wastes. Southerly is a monotonous expanse riddled by creeks and mangrove swamps reaching to the coast, and further south the great Indus River, born one thousand miles north in Afghanistan, flows into the Arabian Sea. The city's population is close to 300,000, its seaport serving a huge hinterland which embraces the whole of Sind, Baluchistan, Afghanistan, the Punjab, and beyond.

Karachi airdrome is, I think, the largest that I know. It is the main intermediate point on all the traffic from Europe to India and the east. Imperial Airways flies frequent schedules all the way to Australia, and K.L.M. to the Dutch East Indies. In military aviation it is, I suppose, the most important headquarters in India, strategically located in relation to the mountain country of the Northwest Frontier, with its troublesome tribes.

In our hurried scheme of things, with the problems of our own special transport uppermost, most of our time "ashore" was spent in and around hangars. More important far than sightseeing was seeing to it that our faithful sky steed was well groomed and fed, its minute mechanical wants cared for. So the geography of our journey likely will remain most clearly memorized in terms of landing-field environments; of odors of baking metal, gasoline and perspiring ground crews; of the roar of warming motors and the clatter of metal-working tools. Such impressions competed, perforce, with the lovely sights of the new worlds we glimpsed: the delectable perfumes of flowers, spices and fragrant countryside; the sounds and songs and music of diverse peoples. . . . Of all those things, external to the task at hand, we clutched what we could.

Those airport interims along the way were jolly with much "ground flying." That's pilot talk. Perched on fuel drums or squatting on concrete aprons in the shade, we listened to tall tales of aviation in far places—over deserts, mountains, jungles—by flying men of the R.A.F., Air France, K.L.M., Pan American, Imperial Airways, Italian military pilots. Stout fellows, all of them, with a rooted love of their craft. Stout spinners of yarns, too, and generously friendly to a female of the species wandering in among them.

One of them at once pressed upon me this clipping from the current Karachi paper:

Airmen's False Teeth Banned
All American Army airmen with false teeth have been ordered to take them out before flying. This is the sequel to warnings issued by Army medical authorities, stating

> that the violent motions of the machine in flight are likely
> to shake the pilot's false teeth down his throat and choke
> him.—*Reuter.*

I agreed with him that this item of news from home was amusing, if not necessarily accurate. And I assured him my teeth were originals.

Speaking of newspapers, there were interviews. One at Karachi I recall especially because it launched me into detailed description of my plane I'd not thought of.

"What a woman pilot wears and what she eats is interesting to other women. But particularly interesting would be a clear picture of the quarters she occupies while flying."

"You mean my cockpit?"

"Exactly. After all, that's your workroom. Beyond your home it's the most important room in your life. From its windows you've seen more of the world on a day's flying than most women will see in their lifetimes."

The person who talked to me like that was a newspaperwoman from Washington—a fine craftsman and individual. That was at Oakland. Then at Karachi, another woman said almost the same things. She wanted to get into the cockpit and sit in my pilot's seat, to see and feel for herself. That I arranged. I told her oldtimers sometimes called the cockpit "the office."

"Since leaving California how many hours have you actually been in your 'office'?"

I figured it up. "Well, that's about 15,000 miles. At 150 m.p.h., let's say a hundred hours."

"Which equals"—my visitor used fingers with her lower mathematics—"about two weeks of working days in a kitchen. And a cockpit is more exciting than a kitchen."

As to that I wasn't convinced. Kitchens can be overpowering. But I was encouraged to feel that nonflyers might be interested in "seeing" my working quarters.

Compared with the single-seated cockpit of my old Vega, the Electra is commodious. The seat of the pilot is at the left, the co-pilot's on the right. On both sides and in front, about shoulder-high as I sit, are windows, with the main instrument board below, and above more instruments.

In all, my "dash" contains perhaps fifty dials and gauges. Those most often used are grouped immediately in front of me. The eye-strain of observing instruments on an angle, or comparatively remotely, is a large factor in fatigue, especially at night. At best, a pilot's eyes have almost too much to do. The constant shift of focus from the horizon, or the terrain beneath, to complicated pointers and dials only a couple of feet away, makes for eye-strain.

One group of instruments has to do with the engines and is completely duplicated for each motor. Then there is another nest of flight and navigation instruments, aids in establishing the ship's position in space and its location geographically. In the first are numbered turn and bank, rate of climb, air speed, artificial horizon and similar indicators. In the latter are compasses, directional gyros, the Bendix direction finder and various radio equipment. In the center of the instrument board is the Sperry Gyro Pilot, the automatic device which can relieve the human pilot.

There are twelve fuel tanks (holding in all 1,150 gallons), six of them in the wings and six in the fuselage, whence complicated plumbing leads to the engines. On long flights there is always a tidy bit of bookkeeping to do, for one should know exactly how much fuel has been used and how much remains.

The receiver for the Western Electric radio is under the co-pilot's seat and the transmitter in the cabin. The main dynamo is under my seat. The radio's cuplike microphone is hung beside the window at the left. Then there is the mechanism of the retractable landing gear and flap control. The flaps are an extension from the lower side of the trailing edges of the wings which act like brakes when landing.

Immediately to the right behind me, the door opens to the fuselage. In a cubbyhole there current charts reside, a thermos bottle, sandwiches, odds and ends. On a shelf at the bottom of the window are a flock of pencils and a notebook in which I write now and then. This haphazard authorship progresses best when the Sperry pilot "spells" me. Just above is the hatch, opening upwards. Usually I exit through it, although one may crawl over the tanks back into the fuselage and use the normal passenger door.

The dimensions of my cubbyhole are four feet eight inches high, four feet six inches wide, and four feet six inches fore-and-aft. If you want to set up those measurements in your drawing room or library, it will help visualize the quarters in which a pilot works. Realize, too, that nearly every inch of floor, wall and ceiling is occupied with equipment. There are considerably more than a hundred gadgets in a modern cockpit that the pilot must periodically look at or twiddle.

And how does all that compare with a kitchen?

Monsoons

From Karachi on June 17 we flew 1,390 miles to Calcutta, landing at Dum Dum airdrome shortly after four in the afternoon.

Low clouds hung about during the beginning of the flight, but these disappeared as we drew near the Sind Desert. Through this great barren stretch rough ridges extended almost at right angles to our course. A southerly wind whipped the sand into the air until the ground disappeared from view in regular "dust bowl" fashion.

We flew along until the ridges grew into mountains and poked their dark backs like sharks through a yellow sea. These acted as a barrier to the sand, and the air cleared somewhat, so we could again see what we were flying over—dry river beds, a few roads connecting villages, and then a railroad.

We had been unable to navigate by railroads heretofore, because none were available, but after reaching central India there were many. There were also rivers and mountains perfectly mapped and easily identified which stand out if the visibility is good.

But on the day we chose to fly, heavy haze curtailed the view after the sand had blown away. Black eagles came flying out of the sky at 5,000 feet. They soared about us lazily, oblivious of the Electra and giving its pilot some very bad moments. How they managed to miss the plane I do not know. I had never had such an experience, and only hoped the birds along the rest of the route would be more cautious in evading the faster-moving machine.

On the sky road to Allahabad we passed not far from Agra where is the Taj Mahal. Tourist-wise, I suppose it is little short of sacrilege to visit Central India and not see the Taj, about which so many thousands of descriptive words have been placed end to end. It would be like a European sightseer dropping in on Buffalo and not viewing Niagara Falls. At all events, Fred and I passed on our way with that dubious distinction.

Below stretched the vast plains of Central India, a succession of tessellated squares of vari-colored cultivation. They appeared like tiles of green and brown and gold, each framed with tiny channels brimming with irrigation water, silver or golden threads reflecting the pale sky or glinting sunshine.

Allahabad is an ancient city on the River Ganges. The surrounding country was whitish in color, and in the haze the trees were black spots. I felt we might be flying over Nebraska after a December snowfall, even though the temperature was ninety degrees at 5,500 feet.

Green mountains piled up beyond Allahabad, and severe rainstorms over them blocked our way. As I tried going between the two, air currents shot us up a thousand feet while I vainly pushed the plane's nose down. Sudden rain engulfed us. After that I gave the squalls more distance, though the air was very rough for miles around.

As the mountains melted into plains a hundred miles from Calcutta, the low clouds disappeared and visibility improved. We could see below many towns and railways and a mosaic of gray and green and tan paddy fields. The country is much wetter than Karachi, with tropical vegetation.

Approaching the metropolis, factories and jute mills came into view, and many villages. These grew more dense, finally merging into the mighty congestion of the city—white buildings glaring in the sun, interspersed with green patches and gardens, dark ribbon thoroughfares, a fringe of docks, and the harbor with its teeming shipping.

Just before we reached the airdrome, more rain caught up with us. When we landed the plane ran through a waterlogged part of the field, throwing up a tremendous cloud of spray which, observers told me afterwards, completely blotted us from view. Soon again there was sunshine, and servicing of plane and personnel commenced promptly on the concrete apron. For Fred and me there was afternoon tea, enjoyed in the shadow of the Electra.

LAST FLIGHT

Driving from the airport to the home of our host, we saw many rickshas. The streets were very wide and thronged with every kind of conveyance and with myriad white-clad figures. Small shops displayed wares next to tall office buildings. Bulls wandered at will on the sidewalks or in the streets, where Shirley Temple was showing in "Captain January."

Calcutta is the capital of the Province of Bengal, its million and more population making much the largest community we had seen, or would see, on our equatorial route—a strange sprawling city of contrasts. Perhaps 10,000 resident Europeans rule its destinies. Though the seat of a considerable university, less than half its population can read and write. Men, I am told, outnumber women by two to one, though why that reversal of the usual was unexplained.

In my notes I read, "The climate is hot and damp." Had I been illiterate as any Bengal beggar, I would have known *that*. "Calcutta has a pleasant cold season from the end of November until March." Because of the Honolulu delay we missed that pleasantness. "The monsoons from June to October are distinguished by heat and humidity." Arriving in mid-June we'd been warned the monsoons might fall upon us momentarily. But we hoped to squeeze through before they struck their stride.

Just what is a "monsoon"? I sought the answer to that question long ago. The books say the name was originally given by the Arabs to seasonal winds which blow approximately six months from the northeast and six months from the southwest. In India the term is especially used for the rain which falls from June to September when the prevailing winds shift to the southwest. The sum total of the situation, monsoonly speaking, was that our course lay southwestward so that monsoon winds were full on our nose; and that no flyer welcomes rains of the density of Indian downpours, especially where there are sudden mountains to slap against and squashy fields to bog down in.

So much for "book learning." Practical experience commenced the following morning. During the hours of the night the monsoon went to work, although only mildly. Its full fury was reserved until we were safely—or unsafely—in the skies.

When we reached the airport at dawn nocturnal rains had soaked it. The ground was thoroughly wet, precarious for a take-off. But meteorologists advised that more rain was coming and that likely we

114

could dodge through the intermittent deluges of the day but that if we remained the field might become waterlogged beyond use. That take-off was precarious, perhaps as risky as any we had. The plane clung for what seemed like ages to the heavy sticky soil before the wheels finally lifted, and we cleared with nothing at all to spare the fringe of trees at the airdrome's edge.

For a time we flew through gray skies crowded with clouds that lowered at us as we passed over the many mouths of the Ganges and Brahmaputra rivers. Below was an agricultural country, green, lush and steaming. The wettest profession in the world is, I think, that of rice grower. Much of the way from Calcutta to Akyab we flew very low over endless paddies. Small figures trailing in the water looked up as we passed over their heads. Some waved hats, others turned back to their work, their every move reflected in a shining flood. Near by their grass houses, ringed by dark green trees, seemed like mushrooms sprouting from luxuriant soil. Now and then water buffalo, resenting the roar of the Electra, would career clumsily across the soggy fields.

Akyab is a picturesque place from the air. Two pagodas, covered with gold leaf, stand out. Near by a creek, so-called in a country where the rivers are enormous, winds through the town, bearing many small boats on its surface. Hilly islands covered with dense jungles lie scattered about. Many of these are really mountainous, and mud volcanoes, I was told, operate on several. How mud keeps boiling during the monsoon downpour I cannot imagine. I should think such rain would quench even a volcano's fire.

The airport is a port of call for most pilots passing this way. It has two runways and a large hangar. Imperial Airways and Air France stop regularly, and K.L.M., the Dutch line, when necessary to refuel or on account of the weather. Speaking of air lines, I have noticed that all K.L.M.'s transports on this side of the world are named after birds, and yesterday, in Calcutta, my Electra shared a hangar with two large four-engined Imperial planes named Artemis and Arethusa—the meeting of the Greeks.

We did not intend to stay at Akyab overnight. Instead we hoped to reach Rangoon at least, and started off from Akyab after checking the weather and fueling.

Once in the air the elements grew progressively hostile. The wind, dead ahead, began to whip furiously. Relentless rain pelted us. The monsoon, I find, lets down more liquid per second than I thought could come out of the skies. Everything was obliterated in the deluge, so savage that it beat off patches of paint along the leading edge of my plane's wings. Only a flying submarine could have prospered. It was wetter even than it had been in that deluge of the mid-South Atlantic. The heavens unloosed an almost unbroken wall of water which would have drowned us had our cockpit not been secure. After trying to get through for a couple of hours we gave up, forced to retreat to Akyab.

Back-tracking, we headed out to sea, flying just off the surface of the water. We were afraid to come low over land on account of the hills. When it's impossible to see a few hundred yards ahead through the driving moisture the prospect of suddenly encountering hilltops is not a pleasant one.

By uncanny powers, Fred Noonan managed to navigate us back to the airport, without being able to see anything but the waves beneath our plane. His comment was, "Two hours and six minutes of going nowhere." For my part, I was glad that our landing gear was retractable, lest it be scraped on trees or waves.

I fondly hoped to have less monsoon on the morrow, but the airport attendants shook their heads and said conditions might not improve for three months. So Fred and I determined to look around for a nice boarding house—in case!

Akyab to Singapore

The next day, June 19, we started again from Akyab, with the hope of getting through to Bangkok, Siam, monsoons permitting. But they did not permit, so the flight ended at Rangoon, only 400 miles away.

This short hop produced even worse weather than that which turned us back on the previous day. Then we had tried unsuccessfully to sneak underneath the monsoon. Those tactics again failing, this time we pulled up to 8,000 feet to be sure of missing the mountain ridges, and barged through. After two hours of flying blind in soupy atmosphere we let down and the bright grain plains beside the Irrawaddy River smiled up at us. Then we dodged about for fifty miles . . . "hooded clouds, like Friars, telling their beads in drops of rain" curtained the sun from view.

The first sight of Rangoon was the sun touching the Shwe Dagon Pagoda. This great structure stands on a considerable eminence and could be seen for miles while the city was still but a shadow on the horizon, its covering of pure gold a burnished beacon for wayfarers of the air.

Shortly after our landing, rain poured down so heavily that it was hazardous to take off for Bangkok, so we decided to stay where we were for a time at least. Fred Noonan and I determined to take one hour off from flying and see something of Rangoon. Mr. Austin C. Brady, the American Consul, at whose home we stayed that night, lent his car and, together with R. P. Pollard, acted as guide, pointing out places of interest. He explained that the road on which we drove to town was called "Mandalay" and actually is "the road to Man-dalay," a day's motor trip from Rangoon.

Of course Kipling's verse ran through my mind. I suppose it's about the best-known song there is. One shudders to think how many tourists have hummed it on the highways of Rangoon.

"That's it," I said.

"What is?" asked Fred.

"Flying fishes."

"Quite." Resignedly.

I elucidated.

> " 'On the road to Mandalay
> Where the flyin' fishes play . . .'

"*Flying* fishes. See? That's what aviators are—ought to be—if they're silly enough to squash around aloft at this season."

Around through the heart of the city we sight-saw. The streets are very colorful, thronged with people of varying hues, dress, habits and language. There are Burmese, Hindus, Moslems, Christians and Chinese. A characteristic they seem to have in common is their love of gay garments. There are many rickshas and gharries, which are one-horse vehicles, the inner furnishings of which I could only guess at as most are shuttered. The ricksha runners all wear—at least when it rains—conical coolie hats made of old kerosene tins.

I noticed some street cars with compartments for women only. These are reserved especially for Indian women, who are forbidden all male association. However, women in general here seem to have more freedom and education than in most places we have been. Many are in business and they have had a vote for many years.

I have seen no fat people. All seem slim and well built. Graceful clothes worn in various styles accentuate their slimness.

After sighting the Golden Pagoda from the air I had to examine it from the ground. To enter, one must be unshod, and plod up long flights of steps, worn by numberless feet before. For the first time on the trip Fred Noonan failed me. He would not take off his shoes and socks and go inside with me. He missed the sight of hundreds of Buddhas of all sizes in little stalls, where drums and gongs were sold. Devotees were kneeling on mats and offering flowers before shrines, with sing-song prayers and strange jeweled ornaments.

There really was a woman smoking a "whacking white cheroot," too. These are made of corn husks filled with leaves and some tobacco, and can be bought in a magnum size for weddings to last three days.

Rangoon is the capital of Burma, twenty miles in from the sea on a deep broad river of its own name, navigable for nine hundred miles behind it. It is a bustling big place with a population of over 400,000. The backbone of Rangoon's export trade is tea and rice. (A backbone of rice sounds odd.)

Moist clouds were our companions as we left Rangoon the next morning, bound for Bangkok, Siam. First, we crossed the upper reaches of the Gulf of Martaban, flying over Moulmein, beside whose pagoda in other days Tommy Atkins left his Burma girl a-settin', looking lazy at the sea. A great range of mountains extends north and south along the western border of Siam, separating it from the long arm of Burma that reaches down into the Malay Peninsula.

Through squally weather we climbed to 8,000 feet and more, topping this mountain barrier. On its eastern flanks the clouds broke and there stretched before us a dark green forest splashed with patches of bright color, cheerful even in the eyes of a pilot who recognized in all the limitless view no landing place. The country fell away gradually to the east, the hills flattening out into heavy jungle. Then we crossed the Mei Khlaung River, with little villages scattered along its banks, the wide expanses of irrigated land burdened with rice crops.

Bangkok itself lies in a vast plain with mountains in the distant background. The Buddhist temples, with their colored tiled roofs and gilded spires, set off the city's skyline picturesquely, as one sees it from the air. Bangkok was once called "The Venice of the Orient," when the Me Nam River, on which it clusters, was its main street, supplemented with a system of canals. Those watery thoroughfares have largely been replaced long since by dry-shod streets. There are open-front wooden shops nestling next to modern concrete structures. Business is chiefly in the hands of Chinese, Indians and Europeans. More than eighty per cent of the Siamese people, I was told, are in agriculture, most of the remaining population being more or less directly connected with Government service.

After refueling at Bangkok (the airport was one of the best we encountered) we started for Singapore, more than 900 miles away, on a course south toward Alor Star, in the Malay States, across the Gulf of Siam. I felt as if I were dreaming, to be flying over such fabulous waters, with the shores of Siam on the right and Cambodia on the left. As we wound southward along the eastern coast of Malay and then across the peninsula to Alor Star, there looked up from the charts stretched out on my knees marvelous names like Bang Taphang, Lem Tane, Koh Phratnog.

The sea, really mauve, melted into a blue sky with companies of little white clouds marching through it. A fairer day could not have been. The monsoon and its perversities were well behind us. Fred Noonan expressed his appreciation: "I thought there was no more weather like this."

A country of green mountains opened before us as, following along one of whose sweet valleys stretching from sea to sea, we slid across the narrow part of the land. We checked over Alor Star airport but did not stop, and headed for Singapore. I chose to hug the western shore, for there were thunderstorms over the mountainous middle way.

Along that day's route I was interested to see charming towns which looked from the air much like those at home. Many had familiar white circles in emergency and regular landing areas, but, unlike those in the United States, few buildings displayed community names on the roofs to help flyers locate exact position.

The fields and valleys were upholstered with a deep-piled green jungle in an unbelievably continuous covering made by separate trees. There were gashes in the verdant carpet of the hills and lowlands, where the roads of rubber plantations and tin mines challenged the forest. But the green growth is unconquerable. Given its head, it swallows up man's puny scratchings almost overnight in the hungry way that jungles have.

Then Singapore. The vast city lies on an island, the broad expanses of its famous harbor filled, as I saw them from aloft that afternoon, with little water bugs, ships of all kinds from every port. Below us, an aviation miracle of the east, lay the magnificent new nine-million-dollar airport, the peer of any in the world. As a reminder that this was indeed the east, when I shut off the engines music from a near-by Chinese theater floated up to greet us. West is west, and east is certainly east. The barren margins of our isolated western airports could scarcely assimilate such urban frivolities.

From the standpoint of military strategy, Singapore is pre-eminent in the Far East. Today, less than one hundred years old, it is the tenth seaport city in the world. Yesterday it was a jungle, its mangrove swamps shared by savage Malay fishermen, tigers and pythons; today it is the cross-road of trade with Europe, Africa, India, Australia, China and Japan. Tin and rubber are the mainstays of its export.

Though we did not sight them, there were two transport planes that day on the same route which we flew. The Imperial Airways machine left Rangoon first and the K.L.M. Douglas at daybreak. Our Wasp-motored Lockheed left fifteen minutes later. All stopped at Bangkok, then followed different courses to Singapore. We arrived there first, at 5:25 P.M., local time, because we cut straight and did not stop along the way. The next day the same caravan was due to leave at dawn for points south.

First to welcome us when we landed were Monnett B. Davis, American Consul General, and Mrs. Davis. They had courage enough to take us for the night, even after I explained our disagreeable habit of getting up at three in the morning and falling asleep immediately after dinner.

Down Under

From Singapore early in the morning we headed for Java. Our course first lay over the open sea, then along the westerly shores of Sumatra, finally cutting deep across its southeast portion. In the first hour of flying we crossed the equator for the third time on our air voyage and definitely passed "down under" into the nether world of Australasia.

The landscapes of the southern hemisphere were beautiful to look upon, but from a pilot's standpoint the dense jungles and mangrove swamps fringing the sea were not reassuring as emergency landing places. We passed above countless tiny islands, glowing emeralds in settings of turquoise. Then the hazy contours of the mountains of Java rose from the tropic sea and gradually the enchanting loveliness of this island world took form. A thousand tiny islets cluster along the Javanese coast. Some are covered with a heavy growth of palms that crowd down to the water's edge. Others are outlined with narrow ribbons of beach, separating the deeper green of their verdure from the exquisite turquoise tones that mark the surrounding shallow water, which in turn merge into darker blue as the waters deepen. The white sails of tiny fishing craft flashed in the sunlight. . . . What with all that lovely world to look at, it required concentration for a pilot to attend to her knitting, which is to say, her horizon and her instruments.

From the garden that is Java rise the immense cones of volcanic mountains. Northward, in low-level regions of India, we had seen much rice cultivation but no such paddy region as this. Here whole countrysides appeared tied like Christmas packages with tawny ribbons of irrigation water, each separate pondlet contained in a diked square of its own, the whole far-reaching grid stretching away to the mountains and even climbing up their sides in a system of stairlike terraces.

Bandoeng is an enchanting place perched among densely wooded mountains. There, apparently, everything horticultural is possible, from tea and coffee to European garden vegetables, from spices to flowers. By the way, eighty percent of the world's output of quinine is grown in Java. Not that there is need for it locally, for Bandoeng has a reputation for a delightfully cool and healthful climate. After a too-brief acquaintance with its attractions I find no reason to question the assertion that it "is one of the modern model cities of the world."

By the way, just an hour after our arrival in Bandoeng a telephone call from New York reached me. It seemed slightly miraculous. I felt as if I might have just dropped into the airport at Cleveland and found a call in Major Jack Berry's office. Jack would probably say, grinning: "G. P. wants you to check in."

After my plane had been comfortably put in its hangar and K.N.I.L.M. (a local organization, sister company to Netherlands Airline, famed "K.L.M.") mechanics had begun their inspection, I went for an inspection trip myself. My first objective was an active volcano, to the crater rim of which one can drive in half an hour up a beautiful mountain road where many people journeyed. Some were laughing and chatting, others were carrying baskets and varying loads, not often on their heads as heretofore, but on poles over their shoulders. Rice fields in terraces bordered the road and on the steepest mountainside I could see cultivated patches. Surely no indolent people farm in such a way.

At 5,000 feet the trees began to dwarf and the vegetation became less dense. At 6,500, only scrub trees which breed in arid soil persisted. I could smell sulphur fumes for some time before rounding the last curve leading to the lower edge of the pit. Hundreds of feet below, emerald water had collected in a pool at the bottom. Here and there jets of yellow-white steam issued from crevices. While the last eruption was in 1910, a volcanologist still lives near and every day takes temperatures for signs of renewed activity.

In his walks he is always preceded by two dogs. They are rated government employees and receive a stated amount each week for their services. They are the first to be exposed to dangerous gases and safeguard their master's life by being first affected. One dog has been three times overcome, and so now is retired on a pension, loafing at home while others carry on.

In one section gases have killed trees in the vicinity and overcome such animals as venture near. At the summit I was really chilly. It was the first time since the start of the trip that I had the opportunity to shiver. We put on leather jackets and liked them.

After dining at the home of one of the K.L.M. pilots, for international "ground flying" is one of the few social events our recent lives have permitted, we stayed at a very good hotel. My room was filled with flowers and everything was as neat and spotlessly clean as Dutch reputation prescribed.

On the 24th of June we thought Bandoeng had really seen the last of us when we flew to Saurabaya, 350 miles on our course near the far end of Java. And then we turned around and flew right back again.

At 3:45 A.M. we were warming up the engines at Bandoeng, planning, if all went well, to fly through to Australia. When one instrument refused to function everyone present turned mechanic and set to work to help. But it was not until two o'clock in the afternoon that the distemper was sufficiently cured to warrant proceeding. After that late start we reached Saurabaya when the descending sun marked declining day. In the air, and afterward, we found that our mechanical troubles had not been cured. Certain further adjustments of faulty long-distance flying instruments were necessary, and so I had to do one of the most difficult things I had ever done in aviation. Instead of keeping on I turned back the next day to Bandoeng.

With good weather ahead, the Electra herself working perfectly, the pilot and navigator eager to go, it was especially hard to have to be "sensible." However, lack of essential instruments in working order would increase unduly the hazards ahead. At Bandoeng were the admirable Dutch technicians and equipment, and wisdom directed we should return for their friendly succor. So again we imposed ourselves upon these good people to whom I shall be grateful always for their generosity and fine spirit. A particular niche in my memory is occupied by Colonel L.H.V. Oyen, commander of the air force, H. A. Vreeburg, chief engineer, and so many K.N.I.L.M. personnel to whom I would like again to say "Thank you."

To the cloud of all this delay there was a silver lining. When the ills of the sick instruments had been diagnosed, and technical labors progressed to a point where my presence could no longer be helpful, there was time for a little sightseeing which extended itself to the neighboring city of Batavia, where friends of Fred, Mr. and Mrs. Fadden, urged us to come.

By air Batavia is twenty minutes from Bandoeng, but by car more than three hours. We drove there to see the country intimately, and flew back to gain perspective. Batavia is the capital of the Dutch East Indies. It was once a walled city, but now only a gate remains to recall the days of constant warfare. Near the gate we chanced on the fish market just when the auction of the day's catch was in progress. Most of the fish are wrapped in banana leaves. An old canal runs through the town, and there the natives wash their clothes and bathe. Wherever there are Dutch people I believe one finds canals and the essence of cleanliness.

In Batavia are entrancing treasures for the stranger from the west. Attractive as they were, we could not weigh down the Electra with purchases. To avoid temptation we had a pact to buy nothing at all—shopping must wait for another visit. To this stern rule I made a small exception. It was a sheath knife—a lovely hand-wrought thing bought at a metal worker's little shop. Seeing the fine Javanese handiwork in knives and swords, I remembered the collection adorning the Washington office of our friend John Oliver LaGorce of the National Geographic Society. Its one unbeautiful specimen was a homely knife which flew with me across the Atlantic, bequeathed to J.O.L. I plotted to bear this Javanese purchase at my belt over the Pacific and then offer it to my favorite Geographer.

No one visits Batavia without having ryst tafel; that is, a meal of rice with twenty-one different courses, including curried chicken, meat, eggs, fish, relishes, nuts, vegetables, all borne in by a line of waiters. To this custom we were no exception. After enjoying the feast I was filled with housewifely determination to reproduce ryst tafel myself, adjusted to the limitations of California marketing environment and certainly pared down as regards servitors. In the solo hands of Fred, our Filipino boy, the effort will at least be more personalized.

Finally on Sunday, June 27, we left Bandoeng. I had hoped to be able to keep on to Port Darwin on the northern coast of Australia. But the penalty for flying east is losing hours. Depending on the distance covered, each day is shortened and one has to be careful to keep the corrected sunset time in mind so as not to be caught out after dark. For instance, between Koepang and Australia there is a loss of one and a half hours.

So, as our landing in Koepang five hours after our start was too late to permit safely carrying on to Darwin that day, we settled down overnight in the pleasant Government rest house, planning to leave the airport at our conventional departure time, dawn.

Koepang is on the southerly tip of the island of Timor, the last outpost of the archipelago of Holland-owned islands which string out southeasterly from Sumatra. As a matter of fact half of Timor is not under Dutch but Portuguese control. In the flight from Bandoeng the first 400 miles was over the lovely garden-land of Java. Then we looked down briefly upon Bali, much photographed island of quaint dancers, lovely costumes, lovelier natives, a well-publicized earthy heaven of *dulce far niente*. Thence we passed over Sumbawa Island, skirted Flores, and cut across a broad arm of the Arafura Sea toward Timor.

As we left Java the geographic characteristics began to change. From lush tropics the countryside became progressively arid. The appearance of Timor itself is vastly different from that of Java. The climate is very dry, the trees and vegetation sparse. There was little or no cultivation in the open spaces around the airport, the surface of which was grass, long, dry and undulating in a strong wind when we arrived.

The field, surrounded by a stout stone fence to keep out roaming wild pigs, we found to be a very good natural landing place. There were no facilities except a little shed for storing fuel. Consequently we had to stake down our Electra and bundle it up for the night with engine and propeller covers. That is an all-important job carefully done; no pilot could sleep peacefully without knowing that his plane was well cared for. Our work much amused the natives from a near-by village. When we had to turn the craft's nose into the wind, all the men willingly and noisily helped us push it as desired.

Then we took time off to see something of Koepang, perched as it is on cliffs with winding paved roads. It has a large Chinese section where apparently, from the diversity of wares displayed, anything from anywhere can be bought. Although the town is on the coast, surrounded by seas so lovely they should make attractive residences for fish, judging by the small size of the local market it appeared that fishing is not important in the Timor scheme of things.

Just before supper at the Rest House a native musician arrived on the front doorstep with a strange instrument made of bamboo and strung with copper and steel wires. It is called a "sesando." We tried to find out what had been the original stringing and whether it was not fiber from a tree. Despite our firm intentions to resist the weight of even extra ounces for the Electra, we were sorely tempted to bring one to Bing Crosby for a present.

We crossed the Timor Sea from Koepang, on Timor Island, in three hours and twenty-nine minutes against strong head winds. We flew over fleecy clouds at a height of 7,000 feet, and possibly this was one reason why we saw no sharks, concerning which everyone had warned us. Great country, this, for "shark talk." Catching them is a business and warning visitors about them an avocation. Even Will Beebe, dean of the school of thought that holds sharks harmless, might wince at the tales told.

The water around Port Darwin was a vivid green as seen from the air on the day of our arrival. Approaching land we saw a small boat in the distance which I insisted was a pearl-fishing lugger. ("Once aboard the lugger and the pearl is mine!" That outrageous observation Fred handed me on a scrap of paper.) Pearl fishing is the main industry—if such a romantic occupation can be so called—of Port Darwin, which is not an industrial town but mainly a government post.

The country of this northern coast of Australia is very different from that surrounding Koepang. There jagged mountains rose against the dawn, while here, as far as one could see, were endless trees on an endless plain.

The airport is good and very easy to find. We were pounced upon by a doctor as we rolled to a stop, and thereupon were examined thoroughly for tropical diseases. No one could approach us or the airplane until we had passed muster. If this work is done at all it should be thorough, and I approved the methods, although the formalities delayed refueling operations.

The customs officials had to clear the Electra as if she were an ocean-going vessel, but that was done with much dispatch. Inasmuch as we had little in the plane but spare parts, fuel and oil, the process was simplified. At Darwin, by the way, we left the parachutes we had carried that far, to be shipped home. A parachute would not help over the Pacific.

Two things in Australia I especially wanted to do were to meet Jean Batten, its famous woman flyer, and to see a Koala bear. I missed out on both. However, a cordial telegram of good wishes came from Miss Batten, then at Sydney.

In the afternoon Fred Noonan and I met C.L.A. Abbott, Administrator of the Northern Territory. He issued cordial invitations for various pleasant functions but, alas, we could not be very social as at dawn we were to end our so-brief stay on the fringe of our fifth continent and shove off easterly, homeward bound.

Lae

Lae, New Guinea, June 30th. After a flight of seven hours and forty-three minutes from Port Darwin, Australia, against head winds as usual, my Electra now rests on the shores of the Pacific. Beyond the Gulf of Huon the waters stretch into the distance. Somewhere beyond the horizon lies California. Twenty-two thousand miles have been covered so far. There are 7,000 more to go.

From Darwin we held a little north of east, cutting across the Wellington Hills on the northern coast of Arnhem Land, which is the topmost region of Australia's Northern Territory. The distance to Lae was about 1,200 miles. Perhaps two-thirds of it was over water, the Arafura Sea, Torres Strait and the Gulf of Papua.

Midway to New Guinea the sea is spotted with freakish islands, stony fingers pointing towards the sky sometimes for hundreds of feet. We had been told the clouds often hang low over this region and it was better to climb above its hazardous minarets than to run the risks of dodging them should we lay our course close to the surface.

Then, too, a high mountain range stretches the length of New Guinea from northwest to southeast. Port Moresby was on the nearer side, but it was necessary to clamber over the divide to reach Lae situated on the low land of the western shore.

As the journey progressed we gradually increased our altitude to more than 11,000 feet to surmount the lower clouds encountered. Even at that, above us towered cumulus turrets, mushrooming miraculously and cast into endless designs by the lights and shadows of the lowering sun. It was a fairy-story sky country, peopled with grotesque cloud creatures who eyed us with ancient wisdom as we threaded our way through its shining white valleys. But the mountains of cloud were only dank gray mist when we barged into them; that was healthier than playing hide-and-seek with unknown mountains of terra firma below. Finally, when dead reckoning indicated we had traveled far enough, we let down gingerly. The thinning clouds obligingly withdrew and we found ourselves where we should be, on the western flanks of the range with the coastline soon below us. Working along it, we found Lae and sat down. We were thankful we had been able to make our way successfully over those remote regions of sea and jungle—strangers in a strange land.

Lae is situated in a corner of a great gulf by a winding river. It is the headquarters for the Guinea Airways Company, which has made an outstanding record for flying passengers and mining equipment into the inaccessible goldfields. Tons upon tons of the heaviest machinery, used in the operations, have been transported by their planes. In fact, no other means exists, and probably without aviation much of the gold would have remained indefinitely in "them thar hills."

Considering the extraordinarily difficult terrain, I think the pilots here have done as notable work as any in the world. The landing field at Lae is one long strip cut out of the jungle, ending abruptly on a cliff at the water's edge. It is 3,000 feet long and firm under all conditions. There are hangars, but a number of planes have to be hitched outside. I noticed all these were metal ones. In regular service here is another Electra, sister to my own.

We stayed at a hotel, a recent addition to a community which itself did not exist a dozen years ago. I am told that about 1,000 Europeans live along the gulf. How many natives I do not know. No inland villages are visible from the air. I should think it would be impossible to find one in the dense growth.

Most noticeable along the shores are villages built out in the shallow waters. Oblong thatched-roof edifices perch precariously on stilts of piling driven into the mud. In the amphibian settlements groups of two or three of the cigar-like huts nestle together, sharing a common platform in front. Most noticeable on landing were native men with peroxide-bleached hair, the sun-tan effect on their heads being striking to a degree. Perhaps the native women also bleach, but of them I saw little. Men alone seem to be engaged in chores inside and outside their homes.

Everyone has been as helpful and co-operative as possible—food, hot baths, mechanical service, radio and weather reports, advice from veteran pilots here—all combine to make us wish we could stay.

However, tomorrow we should be rolling down the runway, bound for points east. Whether everything to be done can be done within this time remains to be seen. If not, we cannot be home by the Fourth of July as we had hoped, even though we are one day up on the calendar of California. It is Wednesday here, but Tuesday there. On this next hop we cross the 180th Meridian, the international dateline when clocks turn back twenty-four hours.

July 1st. "Denmark's a prison," and Lae, attractive and unusual as it is, appears to two flyers just as confining, as the Electra is poised for our longest hop, the 2,556 miles to Howland Island in mid-Pacific. The monoplane is weighted with gasoline and oil to capacity. However, a wind blowing the wrong way and threatening clouds conspired to keep her on the ground today.

In addition, Fred Noonan has been unable, because of radio difficulties, to set his chronometers. Any lack of knowledge of their fastness and slowness would defeat the accuracy of celestial navigation. Howland is such a small spot in the Pacific that every aid to locating it must be available.

Fred and I have worked very hard in the last two days repacking the plane and eliminating everything unessential. We have even discarded as much personal property as we can decently get along without and henceforth propose to travel lighter than ever before. All Fred has is a small tin case which he picked up in Africa. I notice it still rattles, so it cannot be packed very full.

Despite our restlessness and disappointment in not getting off this morning, we still retained enough enthusiasm to do some tame exploring of the near-by country.

We commandeered a truck from the manager of the hotel and with Fred at the wheel, because the native driver was ill with fever, we set out along a dirt road. We forded a sparkling little river, which after a heavy rain, so common in the tropics, can become a veritable torrent, and drove through a lane of grass taller than the truck. We turned into a beautiful cocoanut grove before a village entrance. The natives grow the cocoanuts mostly for their own use and few are exported from here for the commercial markets.

The village was built more or less around a central open plaza. All huts were on stilts and underneath the dogs and pigs hold forth. We were told that the natives train pigs as "watchdogs." Fred said he would hate to come home late at night and admit being bitten by a pig!

Some of the huts had carvings around under the eaves, grotesque colored animals and crocodiles being the most numerous. They reminded me of the work encountered in some parts of Africa.

In the village were several native women, almost the first I had seen, as women here are very much out of evidence. One was bending over a small black cooking vessel from which protruded two enormous cabbages. I also noticed a number of familiar-looking vegetables, which are grown hereabouts, but much of the food used is imported.

My only purchase at Lae besides gasoline has been a dictionary of pidgin English for two shillings. It was well worth the price to discover that all native women are called Mary. I had some difficulty in understanding why "to sew" should be "sew-im-up."

The natives have their own names for everything. For instance, airplanes are called "balus," or "birds." Small planes merit only "bai nutung," or "insects." My plane has acquired special distinction over other metal ones here, which have corrugated surfaces. The Lockheed is smooth and to the native resembles tins in which certain biscuits are shipped from England. Therefore it is known as the "biscuit box."

New Guinea is a country subject to earthquakes and I was told that a 'quake only a year ago shifted a considerable area of shore into the bay, forming the present tiny harbor. They told us that much of the land is really only silt, held together by tangled undergrowth. Along the rivers pieces of "land" sometimes break off and, as islands, float hundreds of miles to sea before disintegrating. Now and then animals are trapped on them.

Then, of course, there is the ever-present jungle to lure one into exploring. I remember the tales told me by Osa and Martin Johnson of their early adventures in New Guinea. That, I think, was their first expedition together, when the hinterlands of the island were full of mystery, not to mention head-hunters, pigmies, and practicing cannibals. Like desert or sea, wild jungle has a strange fascination. I wish we could stay here peacefully for a time and see something of this strange land.

Not much more than a month ago I was on the other shore of the Pacific, looking westward. This evening, I looked eastward over the Pacific. In those fast-moving days which have intervened, the whole width of the world has passed behind us—except this broad ocean. I shall be glad when we have the hazards of its navigation behind us.

By Wireless to the Herald Tribune

LAE, NEW GUINEA, *July 2 (Friday).—Amelia Earhart departed for Howland Island at ten o'clock today beginning a 2,556-mile flight across the Pacific along a route never traveled before by an airplane.*

Miss Earhart's Wasp-motored Lockheed Electra plane made a difficult take-off with ease, but it was only fifty yards from the end of the runway when it rose into the air.

       *   *   *

ABOARD CUTTER "ITASCA" *(off Howland Island), July 2 (AP)—United States sailors and Coast Guardsmen set watch tonight along one of the loneliest stretches of the earth's surface to guide Amelia Earhart on the longest, most hazardous flight of her career. The* Itasca *and the cutter* Ontario *awaited word of her take-off from Lae for Howland Island, an almost microscopic bit of land representing America's frontier in the South Pacific.*

I end A. E.'s book with a paragraph reproduced from a letter she wrote me before a dangerous flight—a letter to be read if it proved to be Last Flight.

G.P.P.

Please know I am quite aware of the hazards I want to do it be-cause I want to do it. Women must try to do things as men have tried. When they fail, their failure must be but a challenge to others.

COURAGE

Courage is the price that life exacts for granting peace.
The soul that knows it not, knows no release
From little things;

Knows not the livid loneliness of fear
Nor mountain heights, where bitter joy can hear
The sound of wings.

How can life grant us boon of living, compensate
For dull gray ugliness and pregnant hate
Unless we dare

The soul's dominion? Each time we make a choice, we pay
With courage to behold resistless day
And count it fair.

AMELIA EARHART